In his ground-breaking book, *With Lucifer On My Side*, Henry Panic reveals the truth about life as a 21st-century Luciferian. Here there are no black masses or blood sacrifices, but the—often raw and viscerally engaging—story of one man trying to live according to very stringent ethics, despite a life beset by trauma, disability and loss. With humour and grit, he takes us through the ups and downs of challenging his Catholic upbringing and adopting what many would consider a darker path. But in fact, what he describes is a life illuminated by a greater light. Never preachy and unconcerned with missionary zeal—there is no intention of converting the reader—and told in direct, everyday language, this book will shine light on what is to the author an ancient truth.

    —Lynn Picknett
        Author, *The Secret History of Lucifer*

WITH LUCIFER ON MY SIDE

WITH LUCIFER ON MY SIDE

HENRY PANIC

Copyrighted Material

With Lucifer On My Side

Copyright © 2019 by Protage Publishing, Inc.
All Rights Reserved.

No part of this publication may be reproduced, stored in a retrieval system or transmitted, in any form or by any means—electronic, mechanical, photocopying, recording or otherwise—without prior written permission from the publisher, except for the inclusion of brief quotations in a review.

For information about this title or to order other books and/or electronic media, contact the publisher:

Henry "Panic" Paniccia
HenryPaniccia.com
@HenryPaniccia

ISBNs
Hardcover: 978-1-7334462-2-8
Softcover: 978-1-7334462-0-4
eBook: 978-1-7334462-1-1

Printed in the United States of America

Cover and Interior design: 1106 Design

DISCLAIMER

I wrote this book outlining certain philosophical and religious theories. I use stories from my life to show how I have upheld these theories or horribly failed them. To be honest, it's mostly the latter. But I wrote those stories remembering the details as best as I could. Regardless, some details have been changed, some character characteristics have been morphed, some situations were compressed, and some names have been changed.

I promise you, if you are reading this book and thinking to yourself, "hmm, that sounds like (insert person you know here)," it is **NOT** them.

It is just a coincidence.

I promise.

CONTENTS

Profiling Lucifer   xi

Two Redactions   xvii

Prologue   xxix

Chapter One: Foundation   1

Chapter Two: The Obvious Connection Between Laveyan Satanism And Luciferianism   27

Chapter Three: Fatal Flaws of the Church   43

Chapter Four: Responsibility and Struggle   61

Chapter Five: Drugs   75

Chapter Six: Humanism   83

Chapter Seven: Determination   95

Chapter Eight: Fear   111

Chapter Nine: Curiosity   123

Chapter Ten: Death   133

Chapter Eleven: Battling My Ego   143

Chapter Twelve: Judgment   153

Chapter Thirteen: Living In Darkness   173

Chapter Fourteen: Freedom and Morality   191

Chapter Fifteen: Life In Light   203

Chapter Sixteen: Know Thyself   215

Acknowledgments   225

About the Author   227

PROFILING LUCIFER

WHO: Lucifer
Lucifer is a Roman name for the "Light Bringer" or "Morning Star." The Morning Star was another name for the planet Venus (mistaken for a star during that time). It was the last "star" seen before sunrise. The Romans worshipped Venus in the same way Greeks worshipped Aphrodite—in fact, they were nearly interchangeable, both being goddesses of love, beauty and fertility.

Aphrodite was probably a recreation of the Babylonian goddess Ishtar (Inanna in Mesopotamia). So if we are to follow the mythological lineage, it would go like this; Inanna, Ishtar, Aphrodite, Venus—and finally, Lucifer.

This is not to say that Lucifer and its predecessors are the same! Each is different in their individual mythology.

ALIASES: The Morning Star, Satan, Beelzebub, the Devil, Leviathan, the Antichrist, Baphomet, Samael, Belial, among others

Of the names listed above, a whomping seven come from Abrahamic religions. Lucifer and Satan are often considered one in the same. (They aren't.) Satan and the Antichrist—as the latter's name suggests, a purely Christian invention—seemed to be tied together like family, so Antichrist could count as another name for Lucifer. The Devil is an alternate name given to Satan, who—as we've seen—is often considered the same as Lucifer. Beelzebub and Samael are names for demons . . . but sometimes also considered Lucifer (Christians really need to have a meeting about this).

In short, Lucifer is a title for all things evil, according to Christians.

LOOKS LIKE: Fallen angel, Baphomet, a goat, a snake, a giant red beast

In Christianity, Lucifer is recognized as the first-created angel. He was also the most beautiful angel, the most powerful angel, but still less than man—who was graced with free will. Lucifer, in exercising his pride, decided to revolt against God. This landed him, and those who fought alongside him, in hell. Lucifer runs hell and it is where spirits who lived evil lives (by Abrahamic standards) go in the afterlife. Therefore, his description as a fallen angel refers to the point he is thrown out of heaven—and falling to earth, then on to hell.

Another allegedly satanic image is that of the Baphomet. The great French occultist and writer Eliphas Levi depicted the image of Baphomet, the devil the Templars were said to have worshipped. He published his first book on ritual magic, *Dogme et Rituel de la Haute Magie (Dogma and Ritual of High Magic)*, actually comprised two separate volumes, *Dogme* (1854) and *Rituel* (1856). The Baphomet makes his appearance in the second volume, *Rituel*.

The Knights Templar, a Catholic military order that began in 1119, were said to worship Baphomet. This was a result of their quick rise to power. Their financial gains were plentiful, and they were present in all major ends of the Christian world (politics, finance, military, etc.). Like all who rise to power, there were plenty who sought to destroy them. King Philip IV of France deemed them devil worshippers and in 1307 sent to have them arrested with an arrest warrant that read, "God is not pleased. We have enemies of faith in the kingdom." Over the next five years they were hunted down, many being killed.

In 1312, Pope Clement V had them disbanded and the remaining leaders executed by burning them at the stake.

The Baphomet is highly popular among Left Hand Path or other occult practitioners. Just what is this powerful and notoriously dark image?

The Baphomet was a sort of perfect representation of all things occult. Masculine and feminine aspects are displayed through the breasts and arms. Both the moon and sun are recognized to reinforce the sense of duality within the image. The words "SOLVE ET COAGULA" are engraved on its arms. The phrase, taken from alchemy, literally means "dissolve and conjoin," referring to the process of breaking something down to its simplest form and rebuilding it as something stronger. It has human arms and torso but a goat's head and hooves, representing the conjoining of man and animal. Everything in the image has its opposite. Every side of nature and spirit is represented.

In Genesis 3:14, God addresses the serpent in the garden of Eden who tempted Eve. He damned the snake to roam the world beneath all other animals, collecting dust and dirt. This is why so many in the western world see snakes as "evil." The Bible never specifically states that the serpent was Satan but given God's ruling over the serpent in the garden, it matches his story.

Upon this, the Book of Revelation 12:7-9 states—

> "7. And there was war in heaven: Michael and his angels fought against the dragon; and the dragon fought and his angels,

> 8. And prevailed not; neither was their place found any more in heaven

> 9. And the great dragon was cast out, that old serpent, called the Devil, and Satan, which deceiveth the whole world: he was cast out into the earth, and his angels were cast out with him"

Combining the story about the snake in the garden of Eden in Genesis with the expulsion of Satan story in Revelation, it is not uncommon to think that Lucifer looks like a snake or reptile of some kind.

When Christianity started to sweep across Europe, battles broke out between them and their new rivals—pagans—some of whom refused to convert to Christianity. Pagans worshipped multiple deities therefore they were perceived as enemies of the Christian God. Over time the Devil's image started to be confused with certain aspects of paganism, typically pagans during ritual practice, where they would pay homage or pray to their gods. All their gods were deemed to be in a pact with the devil, so to Christians Lucifer started to look like the wildest versions of them.

Imagine you are a Christian warrior and you are watching a Celtic (pagan) ritual. You have always been told that these people pray to devils and now you are watching them chant in a circle with a center figure who wears horns from a deer or ram skull. You eventually realize that the center figure is a priest and they are praying to Cernunnos, a powerful Celtic pagan god of beasts who was also called "Horned One." He is typically depicted with a serpent. While there are few records of Cernunnos, one can assume he would be paid homage in times where help with hunting would be needed.

Before you know it, Lucifer gained a set of horns to match his scaley, snake-like skin. The Greeks worshipped Poseidon and he wielded a trident staff. So eventually Lucifer did too. And so forth.

Christianity, just like the Jewish tradition, was skilled in bastardizing other religions, specifically the ones that their enemies followed. We can see the same process when looking at the Jewish creation of the demon, "Lilith." Lilith, a Hebrew word that literally means "demon," was created to bastardize the idea of a feminine deity. Jews were held as slaves by the Babylonians, a nation who followed a polytheistic religion, including a feminine deity named Ishtar. After the ancient Israelites' escape from Babylonian rule, the demonic Lilith was born as a way to demean their previous captors and their beliefs.

TO THE LUCIFERIAN

Lucifer is the embodiment of the life practice the individual Luciferian desires to follow. It is taking from Gnosticism, a life lived like Jesus Christ, or the Buddha, or any other spiritual identity that came to help advance society. There is no desire to rise above your fellow man, sitting higher on the earthly, material plane. That's for your ego. The Luciferian strives to remain spiritually advanced, moving forward as the other Light Bringers have, utilizing the tools of science, spirituality, and self to accomplish a like that is lived like Lucifer.

Lucifer is the way, the practice, the reminder. An umbrella term for us to remember the path we chose to take. Lucifer is neither evil nor avoided. His spirit is embraced, honored, and validated in our lives and practice.

TWO REDACTIONS

"Ya, you know, it kinda reminded me of The Secret."

—Mother Panic

...WHAT?

I paused for a second. *The Secret?* How did this book sound like *The Secret?*

"I don't know what you read that made you think that, but no."

This early review came from my mom two days after its original release on January 7th, 2020. It was the first time I thought I might have made a major mistake with my book.

To start, *With Lucifer On My Side* is a slightly misleading title. Yes, Luciferianism is the main philosophy discussed throughout. All the same, LaVeyan Satanism is regularly discussed as it was the philosophy I followed as a young man. Thelema is in here, too. Buddhism. Stoicism . . .

A more accurate title would've been, *With Left Hand Path Philosophies On My Side*. Or perhaps, *With Occult Philosophies On My Side*.

Given my original state of mind for the majority of the time I was writing this book, it easily could have been entitled *With Drugs*

On My Side, or, *With My Ego On My Side*—or even, *With Insecurities On My Side*. All would've worked as well.

But *With Lucifer On My Side* has a nice ring to it, works well for marketing, and is still relevant.

So I'm keeping it.

The last thing I am going to do is rewrite this entire book. I'm sure the very fact I'm addressing this restructure would have you think otherwise, but I absolutely adore my original version. I went into it taking a major risk both personally and professionally. My philosophical interests weren't something that was discussed a lot throughout my life. If they were brought up I happily joined the discussion as a Satanist or Luciferian, depending on which I considered myself to be at that time. But I also understood that publicly displaying this title attracts a certain slew of questions I'd rather ignore with random people I meet. On top of that, how often do those subjects pop up in normal people's lives?

As you will come to understand, *With Lucifer On My Side* was a real-time project. A great many of the events you are about to read were happening while I was working on this book. The sour influence of life's circumstances flowed—often grossly—into my writing. I hyper-focused on the entire book, which resulted in downplaying parts of stories that should've been explored more, and magnifying parts of stories that weren't as relevant to the whole philosophical point.

Writing this became almost a therapeutic release for the events of that time. And while I can look back on the original and remember what was happening when I was writing certain parts, and smile at *some* of them, the reality is I wrote an autobiography (of sorts) about my life during the two worst years of my life (2017 and 2018). It was hard to think positively during this time. And in reviewing my past, I took a darker approach than I have today. The old versions of this book didn't align with who I am today or who I want to be.

I'm neither asking nor care for your pity but, given that insight, I hope you can better empathize with my reasons for needing to come back and restructure this book.

Ultimately, I wanted the reader's experience to be different.

I've made a couple of distinct changes from the original. I also need to own up to the ignorance I displayed in discussing some philosophical points. I think it's distasteful to sit here and say, "what I meant to say was . . ." so I'll save you my embarrassment (ish).

The stories I use to exemplify these theories haven't changed . . . much. Outside of changing some language to add a sense of maturity that was *desperately* needed at times, it's basically the same. (I started writing this book when I was 25. I'm 33 now. I'm a completely different person today.) Some anecdotal evidence was removed because it was irrelevant to the philosophical point of the chapter. Some stories are further expanded on.

My original understanding of Luciferianism was almost entirely based off Michael Ford's (Ford is a prominent Luciferian author and ritual practitioner) writings and having a slightly skewed perspective towards them (which we will discuss in a moment).

The issue with Ford is the lack of background he presents in his literature. While he has touched on the Hermetica, its individual principles aren't broken down unless discussed in a ritualistic way (I don't perform rituals). The concept of obtaining, acquiring, and earning gnosis is thoroughly discussed through his literature but you don't see much of a historical review. I think philosophies are better understood if we understand the history around them. Ford is a ritual practitioner and therefore discusses Azazel from a ritual standpoint, but never from a Helena P. Blavatsky (the occultist Luciferianism originates from) standpoint. He gives his interpretation of Luciferianism without much of a historic or esoteric foundational basis.

I honestly don't care about hearing someone's philosophical or religious views when they just got married with a new promotion and have a baby on the way. It's easy then. I want to hear about the challenge. The dirty shit. The stuff that would make me not like you. The fuck ups. The struggles. I want to know how you follow your philosophy, your religion, or your god when you're involved in hate groups. I want to know how it works when you're detoxing. I want to hear about it during heartbreak. I want to know how trauma modified you and your life. I want to see the structure get built under the pressures of abnormal circumstances. I want to see you follow philosophy while you're in excruciating pain. When red is the only color you can see. When life is lonely, cold, and dark. Tell me about these experiences. I want to know how your philosophical or religious foundation stood when the world around you crumbles.

I expect the rest went well.

Of course, because there is a balance in all things, this book is **NOT** all dark and gloom because let's be honest, that gets old too. Some truly illuminating stories are beyond these pages. Ditto some even more beautiful theories and philosophical thought.

I'm excited for you join me.

Just keep an open mind.

MY TWO REDACTIONS

1. Luciferianism and paganism have no direct correlation.

2. Luciferianism is **NOT** a religion.

LUCIFERIANISM AND PAGANISM HAVE NO DIRECT CORRELATION

Pagan mythology is littered with Hermetic influence. This is a fact, seeing as the Greek God Hermes, the Messenger of the Gods, was named after Hermes Trismegistus, the powerful sage who is believed to have written *The Emerald Tablet*.

In my ignorance, I thought that any philosophy or myth that extended a Hermetic principle could fall under the veil of Luciferianism, seeing as all the Divine Kings were also men and women who pushed the Hermetic principles through their message. This form of thinking is wrong.

(You will see the term *Divine Kings* periodically mentioned throughout this book so this seems like a good place to discuss this Helena P. Blavatsky theory.

Blavatsky gave the name of *Diving Kings* to *those who helped guide humanity throughout our evolutionary process*. Each of these individuals, who range from mythological beings to historical figures, helped a separate stage of—another Blavatsky idea—the Root-Race.

According to Blavatsky, each evolution in mankind's history is broken down into various sub-sections. Each race was the next step in human evolution. It started not entirely unlike our Big Boom scientific understanding. The *Polarians* are our first Root-Race and they were entirely spiritual beings. The second, *Hyperboreans*, began as spiritual entities but over time became denser and took on early signs of humanity, including the animal forms humanity explored before it became humanity. *Lemurians* were the first to have a physical form, and they were three-eyed giants. *The Atlanteans* are where we start to recognize some names. They are responsible for the Mongolian and ancient Samarian sub-race. And then there's us, the *Aryans*.

Keep in mind that term comes from Hinduism, which was a major part of Blavatsky's extensive, life-long religious studies.

The 6th and 7th race have yet to exist therefore we cannot say what they will be like.

If you caught the obvious hint, I'm happy for you, but don't the Lemurians sound like the Nephilim? And if they are, wouldn't that make Azazel, the biblical leader of the Watchers from the Book of Enoch, their Divine King?

Azazel makes many appearances in this book, and we will cover more of him soon.

In that same way, we have Jesus Christ as a divine figurehead for our current, western humanity. A source of divinity that came to human form to change the way humanity treated one another. To show that the God of Judaism was lost to the real God—the Monad. To show humanity there was another way to reach God, through obtaining gnosis (Greek word for knowledge), specifically esoteric wisdom.

That is from the Gnostic view, which Blavatsky incorporated in her religion Theosophy. We will extensively cover Gnosticism in the first chapter.

Anyway, Divine Kings are humanity's guiding spirits—whether human or of another realm—who help move us along through evolution.

Back to why I was wrong for thinking any philosophy or myth that extended a Hermetic principle could fall under the Luciferian veil . . .)

Luciferianism is Luciferianism because of the path of not only the Divine Kings but also various occult and esoteric philosophies it incorporated—many stemming from polytheistic religions that influenced Judaism. Paganism was seen as a sort of "dark ages" for humanity as far as Blavatsky was concerned. Pagans worshipped earthly gods, or gods created by humanity. Therefore paganism becomes a sort of speed bump in humanity's progression, for Blavatsky.

To further explain the divide, let's look at the Gnostic (Gnosticism is the grandfather philosophy of Luciferianism) *Archons*. Archons were these dumb but violent giants that walked the earth. They helped the Demiurge (the Gnostic sort-of Devil, who nevertheless rules the earth) plague the world with ugly emotional traits and horrific actions. These weren't just "evil" beings by a Christian standard, they were entities that committed the most despicable acts known to man. One Archon is said to have raped Eve (whether it was a *literal* interpretation is up for debate, but still).

The ancient Gnostics declared that there were seven Archons. Each was named after a day of the week. The days of the week are named after pagan gods. So as an extension the Archons took on pagan names.

The Demiurge (and the Archons) is responsible for materialism, envy, and greed. All materialism in Gnosticism was intended to be rejected as the only way to reach salvation. Materialism, like death and ownership, was seen as an exclusively earthly concept. The Gnostics saw the pagan gods as an earthly concept. They were born out of the earth and not the Pleroma (Gnostic heaven). Therefore they were seen as an extension of the Demiurge.

In *Profiling Lucifer*, I explain that Lilith was a Jewish creation intended to bastardize the Babylonian idea of a feminine deity. The way I see it, this is the Gnostic version of that. They bastardized pagan beliefs by naming the Archeons off weekdays. And all weekday names are based off pagan gods.

Point being, the ancient Gnostics were certainly anti-pagan (even if the Church disagreed).

I once stated in the original *With Lucifer On My Side* that I "built my religious structure to be polytheistic." There's a couple of things wrong with that statement.

Luciferianism, as a philosophy, already follows a structure. One that must be adopted in order to follow it properly. Who am I to challenge that? I stand by the idea that no two people will process a philosophy in the same way. Therefore I will never say that neither myself nor anyone else is wrong for interpreting something in a skewed way when looking at philosophy. But through education and critical analysis, my mindset, and—more significantly—my Luciferian practice, has been changed.

For me paganism was (and still is) to be appreciated for the ethos that the myths typically upheld. In them there is an important message for us; Even the gods can be flawed. This is an old idea that seems to be more and more appreciated today. As society enters a new way of life, rejecting the old traditional values that are not seen as important or valuable today, paganism steps in and allows the practitioners to align themselves with a significantly larger basis of living as opposed to the more restrictive Abrahamic religions. By this I mean there is no one way to be a pagan. Modern (and ancient) pagans practiced in the way that made most sense to them, following the paths of the gods that the individual admired most. This is in opposition to Abrahamic religions where there is a direct moral guide you're expected to live by.

You could take the tales of Hercules seriously enough to see how his labors might apply to your own life. Dionysus is a sweetly poisonous but a dear, *dear* old friend. Venus intrigues you more as you start to want a family. I challenge anyone to read traditional Nordic tales of Odin and not appreciate his wisdom, regardless of your current or ancestral culture.

The oral tradition of the Vikings is something to appreciate in and of itself. Norse priests would use different myths to preach to their masses, depending on what was happening in their world. They didn't write their myths. Just passed down stories verbally for thousands of years before the advent of writing and publishing.

Judaism had its own version of this: Some of the Orthodox Jewish traditions were made "holy" as a way for the elders to preach a warning to their younger followers. Jewish leaders said these rules came from God Himself. The most well-known example of this being the milk and meat waiting period which comes out of the *Halakha*, Jewish religious law that evolved over time. It follows Jewish kosher laws and was seen as taboo to cook a baby animal in the milk of their mother.

While kosher laws were important for your health at that time, offering the first healthy way of eating alongside their Muslim brothers *halal*, it is a completely unnecessary practice today in that you can live a non-kosher life and be a healthy individual. To keep the followers of Judaism in line with kosher laws, they said it was a law directly from God.

(Not eating pork was also a part of kosher laws. While Jewish (and Muslim) people would see it as eating a bottom feeder, our modern age has shown us that pork really isn't that quality of meat anyway. Their laws were intended to help a Jewish individual navigate life with ancestorial and religious wisdom, like the Nordic traditions.)

I saw the daemons that Michael Ford (*Bible of the Adversary, Wisdom of Eosphoros*) presented and combined this thought process with my previous understanding of paganism. Throughout the book you will see references to Lucifer, Belial, Samael, Lilith, and Azazel. These are commonly recognized daemons—not demons but guiding spirits—within the Luciferian philosophy as presented by Michael Ford. Seeing as there is a mythology behind each of them, I took that to mean they should be revered exactly the same as pagans viewed their gods.

Even by Ford's standards, this is wrong. And by Blavatsky's standards this is terribly wrong. Pagans worshipped the gods. A Luciferian works with the daemon to elevate themselves in some way, spiritually or not, typically through rituals (which I do not practice—you will see almost zero ritual reference in this book). That isn't the same thing, even if similar in some regard.

Understand, I was raised Catholic. I abandoned it for atheism by the time I was 10 years old. Found LaVeyan Satanism at 13. Started to study pagan mythologies at 21. Found Luciferianism at 23. Coming to Luciferianism from Satanic roots isn't surprising. Coming to Luciferianism after gaining some understanding of paganism isn't surprising. The issue lies in not understanding that I was connecting dots between paganism and Luciferianism that were never really there.

So as you read on and see references to the "gods" I hope you can see them as mythological stories that are aligned with Luciferian tradition, not as actual deities. I want to make this point clear from the start, although it was already addressed at various points throughout this book in its original version.

LUCIFERIANISM IS NOT A RELIGION

Religions bring in a nasty extra component called *organized* religions, and further, churches.

You're going to read all about my issue with religious structures in a later chapter. To summarize, because man builds the structure, it is therefore flawed. Flawed structures can never be the framework for truly moral ideas, polluted as they are by the stench of greed, perversion, and inaccuracy.

It is because of this that Luciferianism is beyond religion, sitting tightly where it belongs in the world of esoteric philosophy.

With religion you will tend to project your own fragilities onto God, "The ALL" (as the Hermeticists would call it), the divine source from which all life came to exist, which is responsible for the cosmos. The entire galaxy. Every source of energy exists because of this idea that there is a singular focal point to all of creation. And whatever that is—let's call it God—is *way* beyond humanity and our petty sins. So why bring a religious structure, a church, into the picture of Luciferianism when Luciferianism is a philosophy that centers itself around a key tenet of truth? Truth involves discovery, which means that some of these ideas we abide by might be changed as new truths become available. The Luciferian should expect this, welcome it, and adapt. That's much harder to do when you have to change an entire religion and its structure every time something new comes into the picture.

On top of this, the grandfather philosophy of Luciferianism is Gnosticism. In the Gnostic Gospel of Thomas it is pretty clear that Jesus Christ thought the idea of a church (or temple) was pointless seeing as you could see God's divinity everywhere. Luciferianism has adopted this same idea.

So let's just leave religion out of it. Luciferianism is a philosophy. One with no centralized dogmatic scripture or deity to worship.

To extend this, theism in the Luciferian philosophy directly opposes certain fundamentals of true Luciferianism. I originally wrote *With Lucifer On My Side* as a theistic Luciferian. Since the release of this book the theism has dissolved. At least, the idea has dissolved in the sense that I do not see daemons as divine "gods." I think Ford was right to present them as daemons (an impartial guiding force in life). Life experience cannot unconvince me that something is there to guide you. All the same, worshipping this, whatever it is, seems silly. My approach today is to recognize it, work with it, listen to it, and go from there. This is the same approach Socrates, the originator of the idea, and Ford would take.

Theism can fall into a grey area within esoteric philosophies. If we understand "God" in the same way the Hermeticists understood "the ALL" are we not believing in God in the sense that we recognize it s/he exists? Is trusting the idea that there is a singular point of divine (or conscious) energy in the world enough to say you believe in God?

Obviously, this is a completely different approach than that of an Abrahamic-religious follower. Believing that God exists—and *just exists*—and worshipping that deity are two completely different things. And that is where the line is drawn.

I cannot see air. No matter how hard I try, when I open my eyes, I do not specifically see air. I see what is behind it. The material world it engulfs. That doesn't mean I don't recognize it is there and serves a purpose. I have an expectation of it to exist. And it has an expectation of me to use it, like all others like me. But I don't worship air. Why would I? It serves its purpose, I serve mine.

This is a good explanation of how I see "god."

I decided to come back a third time to do a clean-up. The first revision was to get the philosophy and story right. This time I am doing my best to improve the writing and give it a positivity lift.

In this third revision I did remove an entire chapter called "Rage." While there was some interesting discussion in there about how I handle my anger, truth is my life is less rage-filled today. To keep it in here just didn't make sense. I'm healed now. A few other chapters were rewritten.

Even after my second release in September 2021, I still wasn't happy with it. I was much happier with it, but by January 2023 I stopped promoting the book. My views, values, and attitude toward some of what was discussed here anecdotally and philosophically has changed.

I wanted to show how these amazing ideas have helped me navigate hardships throughout my life. I believe I accomplished this goal, in some ways. In other ways, I missed my mark. I thought I was healed and I wasn't. My trauma was still a regular part of my daily life.

Today it is not. With that, my mindset has changed. I couldn't have this out there without another run through it. Feeling the shame of a second release makes this one much easier to swallow.

It's my birthday today, August 15, 2024. I'm 33 years old. I started writing this at 25. Seems like a lifetime ago. I was such a different person. In a few ways better, in more ways worse.

Three times is a charm.
Enjoy this final edition.
There will not be a fourth.

PROLOGUE

"To bear misfortunes with a tranquil mind robs hardship of its strength and weight."

—Seneca

THE LIGHT WAS FINALLY starting to show itself through the darkness.

It seemed as if everything in my life was finally becoming illuminated. Work was booming and, at age 25 as a concert promoter, I'd just had three shows with a band who had been in the Top 40 Billboard charts for weeks. I had my first festival concert. I was dropping weight. I was consistently and rapidly beating my personal bests at the gym.

Most of all, I was starting to walk, finally, after every possible setback that could've existed.

Both of my legs were amputated on July 1, 2003. I was walking across the street and got blindsided by a dump truck. As a result I've been wheelchair-bound for 21 years. The amputations are too short for traditional socket prostheses—they would never have a tight enough fit with the socket, or plastic cup into which you fit your stump. Without a tight fit, you're walking on stilts you can't totally manipulate.

Excessive scar tissue was another concern. When I was young and tried to wear prosthetics the skin on my legs would break down. This meant that I had to stop training until it healed, which was at least a couple of months. Then when I started again I'd be back at square one. I did this run a couple of times in my teen years but gave up on the idea of walking until 2014, when I heard about a procedure called osseointegration.

Think of having metal implants deep in your femur almost to the hip, sticking out where your knees should be. They drill into your bone to create space for the implant, hammer it in, rewrap the muscles, and sew you up. This is so you can attach prosthesis directly to the implant, negating the need for a socket. When I stand my weight is bearing directly down onto the bone, like an able-bodied person does when they stand up.

In February 2017 I got the surgery but I had to go to Australia as it didn't have FDA approval in America. I had all kinds of issues with the operation, ranging from a hairline fracture that stopped me from training for six weeks after I left Australia, to the prostheses themselves, to range of motion problems and more. It was all incredibly discouraging though I was still trying to be optimistic.

The American pain specialists were hardly helpful because of the operation being Australian. That's an issue for them for various reasons including malpractice concerns, liability, insurance, and so on. It was like they didn't even want to see me. I'm withering in agony in their offices and was told "tough shit" by doctor after doctor. It took a month after I returned home to get the medication I needed. I understand doctors have to consider if a patient is drug seeking for the wrong reasons (recreational) but I felt this was a pretty valid excuse. They disagreed. So I turned to the street.

I was taking heavy pain medication for six months, as postsurgery I was in permanent agony in my legs. This was due to muscles that had not really been used in 14 years now being worked daily and nerve damage from the surgery itself. My painkiller intake wasn't by any means recreational, it was essential, but either way your body still becomes addicted. At this time I already had gone through five withdrawals—of three-day detoxes each—in that year alone. We're talking mid-February to mid-August.

Still, I was optimistic.

I had just been through my final withdrawal. I was two weeks clean of opiates. I was just starting to walk with forearm crutches and move out of the parallel bars. Which is where you see the majority of your progress. It was a big move for me and every time I walked I became more and more confident in my use of the prostheses. I was given clearance to start wearing them everywhere once forearm crutches came into the picture.

My first outing with them was to the gym.

They were just kind of there though. Outside of some benefits while benching they were honestly more annoying than anything. They would take some getting used to. I was excited when they enabled me to stand up and do pull-ups. It was cool to have other people see me use them. My personal trainer and I decided it would be a regular thing to have them on in the gym.

It was August 17, 2017, and I was working out. The gym I go to is a crossfit-based gym but I powerlift with my trainer. Some of the activities that the crossfitters do impress me. That day they were doing rows with TRX ropes. I had seen this exercise before and told my trainer I wanted to do it with my prosthetics on. He told me to bring them in the following day.

The next day toward the end of my session I put the prosthetics on and got set up. I had boxes at both sides so I could push myself to stand up. We put two 45-pound plates in front of my feet so that if my prosthetics slipped while I was extended, they wouldn't have anywhere to go. We had my trainer in front of me and my wheelchair behind me with another trainer holding it in place.

The plan was for my trainer to give me a light push so I would fall back just enough to have a full extension so I could do the rows. Then my trainer would help me stand back up.

I was nervous but also pretty confident. We believed we'd thought of everything and had a plan for every possible eventuality.

We didn't.

We forgot to account for what happens when people try to fall backward. Try it. You'll soon realize that instinctively you'll flail jerkily forward—and fast . . .

I use the C-Leg 4th Generation prostheses. These prosthetics work through an internal computer chip that dictates when the knee needs to bend. Pressure and weight-bearing on the heel means the leg will stiffen. Pressure and weight on the toe means the knee will break.

I was standing and holding on to the handles of the TRX ropes. My trainer raised his hand to push me back and I lost my balance before he even touched me. I fell backward but swung my hips forward. This caused the knees to break and my entire body swung ahead. I still had hold of the TRX rope handles and kept holding them down, intended to stop me from dropping to the floor. I stopped going forward when my left foot caught on the 45-pound weights in front of me.

My left foot was caught when I swung forward and my femur snapped like a twig. Immediately my trainer was able to pick me up and put me back in my wheelchair. I heard it and felt it but it was only when I saw the osseointegration implant pointing down instead of straight that I realized what had happened.

I knew I needed surgery for my broken leg. With the number of issues I had with doctors in the U.S. I started to freak out about more than just a snapped femur. I thought they might remove the implant—which had taken me three years to obtain. Remove the implant that I couldn't have put back in the U.S. Osseointegration had given me an opportunity I had never believed possible. And while I waited for the ambulance I became convinced they were going to reverse all my hard-won advantage.

The ambulance took me to the hospital, the same one that did my amputations 14 years before, and I absolutely lost it. I was sobbing harder than I had in a decade. Of course I was in pain, but that thought of them removing my implant—a truly seismic setback—and realizing I would be back on pain medication, hurt significantly more. I was finally making progress. I was finally getting some traction in my life, and then this happened.

I felt utterly broken.

The nurses pumped me full of opiates and I kept asking for more. I didn't want to feel anything. I wanted to be entirely numb. As I had months of opiate use behind me whatever the normal dosage is for someone who breaks their femur, I begged the nurse to give me triple. I just wanted it all to stop. I wanted to go back an hour.

I hope you enjoy this book and learn something from it. Thank you.

Henry "Panic" Paniccia
Florida, USA
2024

CHAPTER ONE

FOUNDATION

"There is no higher religion than truth."

—Helena Blavatsky

TO BEGIN, I AM GOING TO LAY OUT the main philosophies that will be discussed throughout this book. Each of these philosophies has played a role in the stories that follow. Not all stories incorporate all these ideas, but every chapter is framed with one (or more) of these philosophies in mind.

I'm giving a quick overview of each of these philosophies. *Obviously,* there is much more to each of them. I expect if you are picking up this book you are already somewhat in "the know." I want you to see this as a quick summary.

If you are a newcomer, understand that my interpretation of these philosophies will be different than yours. The way I put these philosophies into practice and the way you might practice them are probably going to be different. You need to keep that in mind as you read this book. My understanding, my practice, my life is not a perfect representation of these theories—this is just my own experience of living with them.

The main purpose of most of these ideas is to *glorify the individual*. Whether through indulgence, or your True Will, gaining gnosis, or productive achievement, the intention here is to grow. To live to your highest ability. To move through the world gaining a further understanding of these hidden truths and sharing those truths as you move forward. A term Michael Ford, a current leader in the Luciferian philosophy, created for these ideas to embody the above would be—perhaps shockingly to many—"Light Bearer".

I am not the final say on these ideas. I will provide relevant information but how I interpret that information and how you would interpret that information will be different in some way. That's expected. Even encouraged. If you are interested in these ideas, step one is to think for yourself. Make your own judgment. See the life anecdotes I present as situations from which you can look at through a philosophical lens.

Just remember the lens you're viewing this from is mine, not yours.

Luciferianism emcompasses a *large* number of various ancient belief structures and mythologies. But seeing as **absolutely no one** should be reading this as a 'What Is Luciferianism?' book (these brief overviews only touch on each philosophy—the vast majority of this book is about how I practice these ideals), I found it most important to focus on what was specifically important to me. Not all the philosophies mentioned here fall into the occult, esoteric, or Left-Hand Path categories. Objectivism and Stoicism, for example, are technically outside the occult philosophy realm but because they are still important to me they will be given honorable mentions here.

All the same there are entire ends of the philosophy we won't get to here, including Egyptian mythology, ceremonial magick, the Qabalah, and more.

One of the changes I made from my original text was the quote at the head of each chapter. Previously it was from favored musicians.

Now it is a quote from a philosophical leader: LaVey, Aurelius, Crowley, Buddha, and more will head each chapter to give you an idea of which belief system will be featured in the following pages.

GNOSTICISM

Gnosticism is the grandfather philosophy of Luciferianism.

First, Gnosticism comes from the Greek word *gnosis*, meaning knowledge. Gnosticism at its core is entirely about seeking knowledge, specifically hidden or esoteric knowledge. By doing so the Gnostic lives to the highest level of being he or she can—and in their afterlife, they take their place in the Pleroma, or the realm of divine manifestations.

Breaking down the hierarchy, we have the *Monad*, the highest God. The Monad produced *Aeons*, lesser beings born from God. The Aeons exist in the *Pleroma*, which is the totality of divine energies (just think of it as a Gnostic heaven). Out of these Aeons came *Sophia*, the Gnostic name for the feminine divine energy and embodiment of wisdom. Sophia is responsible for the creation of the *Demiurge* (and further, material world), a mistaken creation made out of matter and the soul. The soul is often seen as one in the same as the *Divine Spark*, the part of the Monad that resides in all living beings. The Gnostics believe that all Aeons were created as a masculine and feminine pack—or rather twins of the same divine source. In some forms of Christian Gnosticism, Sophia is regarded as the feminine counterpart to the Christ, his *syzygy*.

Christian Gnostics believe the highest God sent the *Christ*—which simply means 'anointed one'—as a human representation of the Divine. That human is a religious figure known as *Jesus Christ*. To the Gnostics, Christ the spiritual Aeon and Jesus Christ the human being were separate beings living together in the human form. Christ, being an Aeon, a soul outside of the physical realm, was placed into Jesus Christ's being, which happened at his baptism.

The Christ was sent to direct humanity away from the lost true holy tradition. According to the Gnostics—who were very unconventional

Christians—he preached that Jehovah (seen as the Demiurge) must be rejected to reach the highest levels of salvation, or *fullness*, that one could reach. One would go about this through studying and utilizing sources of divine wisdom left across the world. In doing so you could return to the Pleroma after death (and potentially before, as fullness could be reached throughout life) and remain among the Monad.

Non-Christian Gnostics believe Jesus Christ was human who obtained gnosis and spread the message to his apostles. The non-Christian Gnostics—the way the vast majority of Luciferians will perceive Gnosticism—rejected the idea that an Aeon basically possessed a human. To them, no human is higher than any other in terms of Divinity, *unless* they obtain the proper gnosis to achieve fullness, which they believe Jesus Christ obtained. He was a human that reached fullness, not a human in Aeon form, which would make him divine.

Jesus Christ isn't the only important distinction between contemporary Christianity and Gnosticism, though.

Let's review the story of Adam and Eve from the Christian view . . .

One day in the garden of Eden the serpent spoke to Eve. He asked her if she had eaten from the Tree of Knowledge. She replied that she hadn't, for God had told her if she had, she would surely die. The snake replied that she would *not* die if she did so. Eve takes Adam to the Tree of Knowledge, grab a piece of fruit, and eat. Immediately they both feel shame. They realize they are naked in the garden of Eden. God came to them later in the day, furious that they would betray his word.

Same story but from the Gnostic view from the Testimony of Truth in their long-lost texts, now known as the Nag Hammadi Scriptures . . .

One day in the Garden of Eden the serpent spoke to Eve. He asked her if she had eaten from the Tree of Knowledge. She replied that she hadn't, for God had told her if she had, she would surely die. The serpent replied that she would not die, and the "God" who told her this is not God at all, but the Demiurge, a lesser being intended to enslave humanity in ignorance. The serpent told her that by eating from the Tree of Knowledge she would be like God, knowing both good and evil. Eve takes Adam to the Tree, grabs a piece of fruit, and they eat. The jealous Demiurge banishes them from Eden for their disobedience to his word.

This only touches on a small portion of the Genesis story from the Gnostic viewpoint. Eve, for example, is viewed as the superior to Adam—his teacher—and from whom he was created (in almost every other species in the world the female gives birth, but not in Judaism and Christianity, where woman is born from man . . .).

The early church leaders spoke against the Gnostics. In one unsurprisingly unfriendly outburst, one church leader called them devil worshippers, while another one labelled them child molesters—none were sympathetic. Who we call Gnostics today were deemed heretics by the church. They were seen as polytheists and fantasists and therefore against Christianity.

The Nag Hammadi scriptures (found in Egypt in 1945 and including the likes of the Gnostic Gospel of Thomas) are dismissed by the Catholic Church (the largest denomination within Christianity) for a variety of reasons. I find the most interesting reason to be is that the Church will claim the Gnostic scriptures do not paint a Jewish Jesus Christ but rather very much their own, distinctly Gnostic one.

The issue here lies in the Church burying the truth . . . The idea of Jesus Christ as a human being as opposed to the human personification of God—which is the current Church stance and has been since 325 AD—was widely believed and accepted by Christians. The evidence shows that the first generations of Christians saw Jesus Christ as a divine and enlightened person, but still a human being. The Church decided he was divine, not the religion itself. This isn't to take away from the awesome importance of Jesus Christ, as his apostles certainly thought he was divine, but he was still a human being and lived as such.

The reason for the church's decision will be discussed in an upcoming chapter.

HERMETICISM

Hermeticism is the product of two separate collections of literature: *The Corpus Hermeticum* and *The Emerald Tablet*. Both were said to be written by a powerful sage named Hermes Trismegistus.

Hermes Trismegistus is said to have lived sometime around 600-500 BC (there is some debate over whether he existed, but I personally think there's more than enough to suggest he was a real person). He was a powerful sage who was associated with both the Greek god Hermes (Mercury for the Romans, Enoch for the Abrahamic adaption), and the Egyptian god Thoth. The Greek god *Hermes* was said to be the messenger of the gods, carrying forward divine knowledge (beside other responsibilities). The Egyptian god *Thoth* was the god of wisdom, magick, and writing. Both gods—and by extension, Hermes Trismegistus himself—were directly associated with alchemists as they connected humanity and the divine, whether through writing (philosophy) or the elaborate, secretive rituals of their magick.

There are seven Hermetic Principles as per *The Kybalion* (1908). *The Kybalion* was a summarization of sorts for the lessons of Hermes Trismegistus.

1. Mentalism—"The ALL is Mind; the Universe is mental."
   The first Hermetic principle tells us that we are a mental creation of "The ALL." Due to this, all things within our material world are governed by the same universal laws as it as stems from the same singular point of creation.

2. Correspondence—"As above, so below; as below so above."
   This principle exists to show us that there is a pattern that links all planes of existence, which the Hermeticists broke down to three different planes: material, mental, and

spiritual. The most material level influences the most spiritual and vice versa.

3. Vibration—"Nothing rests; everything moves; everything vibrates."
   This principle tells us that everything radiates a vibration. Whether it is a material object or an idea, there is a vibration attached to it.

4. Polarity—"Everything is Dual; everything has poles; everything has its pair of opposites."
   This principle is there to tell us that everything has another, opposite and equal side, like yin and yang, the eternal female and male—though they go much deeper than that. They are the two complementary, balancing forces that underpin all manifestations of life.

5. Rhythm—"Everything flows, out and in; everything has its tides; all things rise and fall."
   This the principle of change. Everything is in a constant state of flux, ever-changing. Even you, as you read this, are changing. You are getting older, more tired as the day passes, and internally your body is working to keep everything in order.

6. Cause and Effect—"Every Cause has its Effect; every Effect has its Cause; everything happens according to Law."
   Pretty self-explanatory. This principle states that there is a reason for everything that happens. Not necessarily fate but, in conjunction with the other principles, it works because the universe follows an order. A rhythm. A "Law."

7. Gender—"Gender is in everything; everything has its Masculine and Feminine Principles: Gender manifests on all planes."

Gender—or rather masculine and feminine elements—exist on a sliding scale. Nothing is entirely on either side. There is a duality of both in all things.

None of this is to ignore the historical and scientific importance of the Hermetica.

Let's go back to the 2nd century AD. Meet Ptolemy of Alexandria (100-170 AD), the astronomer responsible for the *geocentric* theory, which held that the sun, planets, stars, and entire universe, rotated around the earth. This theory was adopted throughout Europe until the 16th century.

Meet Nicolaus Copernicus (1473-1543), the Renaissance era mathematician and astronomer largely responsible for the *heliocentric* theory. This states that the earth, as well as the other planets, move around the sun. The moon rotates around the earth. Copernicus didn't release his teaching until his death, stating he didn't want lesser scholars to fight him. Even then, he simply proposed this as a theory.

What does the heliocentric theory have to do with Hermeticism? *It's where the idea originated!*

The Renaissance brought about a revival of the Hermetic teachings. It offered a new way to understand the world, spirituality, religion, and God. It gave a reason for why humanity seeks God (because we are offshoots of The ALL's divine energy). It gave a rationale for religion, or at the very least, for God. This idea specifically intrigued the intellectuals of that era. And that includes Copernicus, who studied in Rome and Padua, where he undeniably would have been exposed to Hermetic teachings—which were widely seen as electrifyingly exciting by European intellectuals.

The Hermeticists placed great importance on the sun, seeing it as the embodiment of divine radiation throughout our universe. In the *Corpus Hermeticum* there is reference to the idea that the sun is at the center of the universe, and the remaining planets circulate the sun.

Introducing Galileo Galilei, the Italian astronomer who was the first major scientist to turn the telescope towards the skies. This allowed him to prove Copernicus was right. It also silenced the critics of the heliocentric theory who stated if Copernicus was right then the stars would move as well. Galileo argued they were, just slowly. This opened the idea to the vastness of the universe. The world was able to look at stars differently—and correctly. Modern astronomy was born.

Finally, none other than Sir Isaac Newton himself, the English physicist, often regarded as the most influential scientist of all time, as well as the father of physics. Newton brought it all together with the mathematical proof of his three laws of physics in his landmark book, *Principia Mathematica* (1687)—one of the most far-reaching texts of all time. Newton's work directly proved the heliocentric theory, among other great scientific revelations, which opened the way for all the big inventions and discoveries of science that came after. It's no exaggeration to say that Newton's book pretty much created our modern world. Newton, it transpires, was also *directly* inspired by the Hermetica (he was introduced to the Hermetica at Cambridge University, where he studied law).

This idea that an ancient mystical philosophy could project scientific revelations *long* before modern science, adds an important flavor.

As for Hermes Trismegistus . . . perhaps he was indeed a messenger of the gods.

Hermeticism makes it possible for you to use the word "God" and "science" in the same sentence—and it is both philosophically and scientifically true.

Nearly every chapter in this book was written and framed with a Hermetic principle in mind.

BUDDHISM

Buddhism is an ancient Eastern religion that began with Buddha (named Siddhartha Gautama). ("Buddha" itself became a title for any mystically enlightened person.) Siddhartha was prophesized that he would be a great king or spiritual leader. Due to this, his father then kept him secluded in his palace until he was 29 years old so he would never know the horrors of the world. Siddhartha received his first glimpse of the real world by seeing the sick and dead. He decided on that day he would turn to spirituality, realizing his time on this planet was limited.

For the next six years he worked with spiritual teachers and leaders in hopes he could find enlightenment. He decided that mental discipline would be his salvation. He sat under "the Bodhi tree" and meditated. Upon returning to normal consciousness he decided he would be known thereforth as the "Buddha." And so he began his teachings.

Buddhism, while only arguably a religion—it worships no god—is an entire philosophy. While it is extremely relevant to Luciferianism, as Buddha himself was considered a Divine King by Blavatsky, we are going to focus on the Buddhist connection to *minimalism* or living with as few material items as you can.

All suffering you experience in life—according to Buddhists—is because you are attachment to something. The attachment leads to suffering. If you can learn to detach, you can end your suffering.

In its purist form, Buddhism rejects earthly, material objects. To live a life where all you do is try to accumulate gold or and surround yourself with clutter is to waste your life, to the Buddhists. The less detached you are to things, the further you would be to reaching enlightenment. For example, Buddhist Monks live extremely minimalist existences and have for thousands of years. The idea being that you don't need a lot of material objects to live a fulfilling life. You need very few actually.

I discovered this at a young age. I had many possessions. It filled a space—whether physical or mental—but the objects alone never actually fulfilled me. It was what I did with them. I was a young homeowner and I can confidently tell you owning a house sucks, at times. Shit breaks all the time, you're always fixing something, property taxes exist—it's a nightmare. But what isn't a nightmare were the memories I created in that home. The material object, the house, only served as A/C controlled room for the great memories that were made.

I do not live as a true minimalist. Regardless, over the years I have lessened the load more and more. It feels good. Less things to own is less to worry about. The Buddhist concept remains true. My life is undeniably "fuller" than it ever has been and I can guarantee you I have fewer possessions today than any other time in my adult life. With every bag of useless junk I've collected over the years that gets tossed away, life actually feels lighter. There isn't much more to clear out at this point.

The real challenge is learning to detach from *people*. That lesson is much more difficult.

A common Buddhist understanding of compassion is useful as well. It's not presented as love necessarily, at least not in the Christian sense, but rather as, "this is no longer good for me, which means it is no longer good for you. It is in our best interest to cease whatever it is we are involved in so we can both benefit from something else elsewhere." I think this idea is important as it is not based in spite, nor is it based in useless "help everyone you can" ideology, but rather looking at both ends and benefitting both.

True compassion is not only sympathetic and empathetic but also intended to end the suffering of others, for the Buddhists. The above understanding covers all of that for both parties (or more) involved. It is both selfless and selfish, perfectly and purposely blending the two opposites in the same action.

More on the idea later . . .

These two ideas, minimalism and the Buddhist understanding of compassion, will be seen throughout this book.

THELEMA

Philosophies are typically better than those who present them. This is no different with the founder of Thelema—the controversial and flamboyant Englishman Aleister Crowley (1875-1947), whose own mother said he was "The Great Beast 666." Crowley was a member of the Hermetic Order of Golden Dawn before starting Thelema, his religion and/or philosophy. Unsurprisingly, you can find many connections between his writings and Hermeticism (Kabbalah, a Jewish mysticism text, too). A man who said ancient Egyptian Gods—and a non-human entity called Aiwass—communicated with him and revealed the universal laws he then handed down to the followers of Thelema.

Thelema is based around the writings of Crowley. Specifically, his book *The Book of the Law* (1909), also called *Liber AL vel Legis*. *The Book of the Law* came about on a celebration of love and romance . . . his honeymoon in Egypt. (Because nothing says sexy like occultism, of course.) His wife, Rose, was not an occultist but after she watched him fail again and again to invoke a spirit, she heard a noise. Then another. And soon she says Horus, the ancient Egyptian God of the sky, by name and declares he is about to manifest. This catches Crowley's attention—especially as she was very ignorant about Horus—and he decides to invoke Thoth (the Egyptian God of writing—connected to Hermes Trismegistus). Thoth and Crowley decide to invoke Horus on April 9th, 1904, at noon.

The Book of the Law was born from messages Rose received from Aiwass—the entity that was speaking for Horus—on April 10th, 11th, and 12th from noon for an hour. *The Book of the Law* was broken into three different chapters, each told by a different Thelemic god or goddess. *Nuit*, the divine feminine, was the twin of *Hadit*, her masculine counterpart. (Not unlike the Gnostic idea of Sophia and Christ.) And then there's *Heru-ra-ha*, the Crowned One, and the Lord of the new Aeon—of which, Crowley declared, Thelema was the start. One where humanity would flourish spiritually.

Is it a religion? A philosophy? I don't know. And neither do the Thelema communities, which are popular within occult circles reaching across the globe. Crowley wanted the followers to use Thelema in whatever way was best suited to them, religion or philosophy. Thelema itself is a Greek word for "will." Crowley often referred to it as a "law," one that the individuals on a spiritual journey could explore on their own terms. This particular law allows the practitioner to recognize their own inner divinity and to act on their own accord, or their "True Will."

In regard to someone's "True Will," Crowley stated, "What is necessary is not to seek after some fantastic ideal, utterly unsuited to our real needs, but to discover the true nature of those needs, to fulfill them, and rejoice therein."

To illustrate Crowley's take on True Will, allow me to introduce *Clueless* Daria.

Daria is a run-away who just turned 18. She's been on her own since she was 16 years old. She is headed for Los Angeles, California, hoping to be a famous actress. She is driven, bold, and will see an impressive level of success throughout her career. She will "make it," as some say. But she will always want more, always crave more, unable to savor her accomplishments in the slightest, and eventually this is what causes her downfall.

Daria's "fantastic ideal" was to be famous. She wanted the praise and love and affection given by fans for stars' acting talent and charisma. Seeing as she was disowned by her junkie parents, who didn't want her as much as they wanted their next hit, she was going to make herself wanted by everyone. She would be a sex symbol the men would drool after and adorn herself in the highest fashion and beauty to attract women, many of whom are just like her. But none of this helped satisfy her real needs—unconditional love and acceptance.

As a result, she becomes her parents, losing copious amounts of hard-earned money and falling victim to heroin. She never feels happy or fulfilled. She never discovers the true nature of her needs.

Ouch . . . Let's see *Thelemite* Daria.

Daria is a run-away who just turned 18. She never had a family, or at least never had one that appreciated her as much as she deserved.

While she was dismissed by them, she never dismissed herself. She knew she had the raw talent and drive to make it in the entertainment industry and set out for California to do just that. After a couple years of serious dedication she was given her first real chance.

Those same feelings of dismissal she received when she was kicked out of her home at 16 fueled her hard-work ethic. Seeing her parents succumb to drugs and poverty made her swear she would never end up like that. While the entertainment industry paved every way for her to follow in the footsteps of her parents, she knew that the real love and acceptance she sought after wasn't provided through a syringe, but in genuine connection with others.

As a result, she "made it." Throughout her career she was praised as a bold, authentic, and a genuinely hard-working woman loved and truly appreciated by many. Through her life and career she felt truly fulfilled, something her childhood never offered her but she knew she was worth receiving.

In one version, Daria is chasing an ideal without any real coping mechanisms or even basic self-regard. In the other, realizing her true worth and potential, she is challenging herself to live to her True Will.

In *The Book of the Law*, Crowley states "every man and every woman is a star." By this he meant that every man and woman should view themselves as an individual with a gravitational pull. The individual, specifically in their body, is the center point of their Will. As a result, all things that expand from this singular point is a radiation caused by them. Their "light" illuminates the world because they are this "star," this point of divinity. If you are always acting in accordance with your True Will, then your "star" will shine with a true uniqueness.

For all its cryptic language, *The Book of the Law* and Crowley himself built Thelema to be a philosophy that could and should be differently viewed by each person. No two Thelemites practice the same way—which makes perfect sense as no two individuals are the same. Crowley wanted an individual to understand their personal perspective was important, something to be valued, which would dictate how they viewed Thelema—and further, how they practiced it.

Due to this, I want to remind people that this is simply *my* understanding of these ideas. You could read the same material and have an entirely different comprehension of it. It is not my job to interpret these ideas for you, nor is that my goal. I am simply explaining what they mean to me.

SATANISM

Before we can get to the details of modern Satanism, we need to discuss its founder, Anton Szandor LaVey (1930-1997).

In 1966 LaVey established Satanism as a formal religion with the Church of Satan, with its headquarters originally in California, now in New York. In 1969 he published *The Satanic Bible* and in the years that followed *The Satanic Rituals* (1972), *The Satanic Witch* (1971), *The Devil's Notebook* (1992), and more.

LaVey decided to establish Satanism as a formal religion to fight the hypocrisy he'd seen during his time as an organ player in an evangelical church. He'd also worked as a carnival employee. He would see the same men lusting after women at the carnival, then going to church on Sunday to repent. As he properly saw it, these men were not truly sorry. They were trying to buy God's good graces after willingly and happily sinning. So, as LaVey once said, "if you're going to be a sinner, be the best sinner on the block!"

His idea was to embrace these carnal desires and to stop worrying about what some grandfather-lookalike in the sky has to say about it. With this realization came his philosophy and his take on Satanism.

To understand modern Satanism, we need to look at what Satan actually means to the Satanist. To do this we are going to examine LaVey's Nine Satanic Statements from his book *The Satanic Bible*—

1. Satan represents indulgence instead of abstinence!

2. Satan represents vital existence, instead of spiritual pipe dreams!

3. Satan represents undefiled wisdom, instead of hypocritical self-deceit!

4. Satan represents kindness to those who deserve it, instead of love wasted on ingrates!

5. Satan represents vengeance, instead of turning the other cheek!

6. Satan represents responsibility to the responsible, instead of concern for psychic vampires!

7. Satan represents man as just another animal, sometimes better, more often worse than those that walk on all-fours, who, because of his "divine spiritual and intellectual development," has become the most vicious animal of all!

8. Satan represents all of the so-called sins, as they all lead to physical, mental, or emotional gratification!

9. Satan has been the best friend the church has ever had, as he has kept it in business all these years!

The Satanist does not believe in an actual devil. The only people who believe in Satan as the adversary to the Abrahamic God are those who believe in the Abrahamic God. To the Satanist, Satan represents all of the above and then some. Satan is the rebellion. Satan is the adversary. The lone wolf. But at no point does the Satanist see Satan as "evil," or even more so, something to be ignored, dismissed, or shamed.

I found Satanism when I was 13. I remember my obsession with *The Satanic Bible*. I could not stop reading that book—in part because I could only understand so much of it at that age. Still, I adopted the title of Satanist and wore it proudly until I started to explore paganism when I was 21. And even then, I still held onto that title for another couple of years—until I found Luciferianism. (As we will see, this is distinct from Satanism.)

Satanism was a pivotal landmark in my development as a young man. I followed it, perhaps a bit rigidly at times, and found it exceptionally useful. The idea that I was only following an ego-based belief system didn't present any problems to me. I didn't see much of an issue until I started researching various pagan myths. By the time I found Luciferianism I saw Satanism differently.

The issue with Satanism is that it doesn't cover the entire spectrum of life. There's more to life than just seeking pure indulgence. One of the difficult things I found in my younger years was that my understanding of discipline was limited, in part because I didn't understand that indulgence could be taken too far.

Today I look at Satanism differently than when I was younger. I still see it as an important philosophy. A great idea. But it only covers half of the development I want to seek out throughout my life. Even so, there will still be many references to Satanism and LaVey throughout these pages.

OBJECTIVISM

Anton LaVey (in part) pulled from the philosophy of the highly controversial Russian-American commentator Ayn Rand (1905-1982), a belief system called *objectivism*. Satanism and objectivism share numerous similarities, though LaVey did add his own flair. Objectivism can be summarized best by the idea that selfish is not a bad word and in being selfish we offer the best of ourselves to the world around us.

Everyone is selfish, though the concept of selfishness has been largely distorted. If you ask most people what being selfish means, most will probably reply something similar to being manipulative. The two terms are not one and the same. Being selfish means we do something for our own benefit, our own satisfaction, our own will. This is very open-ended and it should be, as an individual's degree of selfishness can stretch across all actions performed, past and present. Manipulation is exploiting someone else for your benefit. How these two terms came to mean the same is probably a result of Judeo-Christian attitudes. With Judaism we saw the idea of selfless sacrifice for God, such as fasting. With Christianity we saw the idea of loving your neighbor as you love yourself and even to love those who persecute you. Jesus' ideas are intrinsically a rejection of selfishness because they urge you to give time and energy intensely to others instead of focusing on your own well being.

Objectivism covers much more than the idea of selfishness. Rand explained objectivism as *"the concept of man as a heroic being with his own happiness as the moral purpose for his life. With productive achievement as his noblest activity and reason as his only absolute."* In layman's terms, an individual's happiness should be at the forefront of their lives. Their purpose is driven by their own desires. Well, this sounds like everyone, right? Doesn't everyone do the things that make them happy? Isn't that kind of the point of life?

I think most people would say yes because it sounds good—but whether or not the majority's actions reflect this idea is debatable.

Additionally, Rand placed an importance on understanding reality through an analysis of *reason*—the most important value in objectivism. She believed being rational was key to an individual's contribution to the world. To be reasonable or rational, you have to think for yourself, one of the basic premises of Satanism.

Some critics of objectivism suggested that her philosophy rejected the idea of a communal spirit. While I understand the thought process, I think it is important to look at Ayn Rand herself. She grew up in communist Russia, though her philosophy does focus on the individual; whereas communism and other similar ideas focus, at least in principle, on the majority. Her own rational thoughts helped her realize that communal spirit does not come before the individuals. In this way she emphasized the importance of utilizing your rational thinking to help define the very philosophy itself. That isn't to say objectivism is anti-democracy, because it isn't, but the emphasis is on the individual. This is where the negative interpretation of selfishness comes into play.

Tying objectivism into Satanism is pretty easy once you understand the basics. Satanism is entirely about the individual's will, with a couple of guidelines to adhere to—which is also similar to Thelema.

STOICISM

Stoicism comes down to one simple idea . . .

If it is happening to you, it is because it is your fate to have it happen. It is your responsibility to endure it with strength, integrity, and without complaint. You are expected to "weather the storm" as a sturdy man or woman, one who accepts that whatever hardship they are dealing with is something they can overcome. This isn't meant to ignore your emotional side, as the stoics were highly emotionally intelligent individuals. There's this idea that stoicism rejects emotion and it couldn't be further from the truth. Stoicism promotes controlling yourself and, by extension, your emotions. It elevates the idea that your emotions shouldn't control you.

As far as the stoics were concerned, if you were fated to suffer an unfortunate event, fate has given you the tools you need to overcome the hardship—and even come out on top.

Personally, I'm not crazy about the idea of fate. For the same reason I always found Calvinism to be such a strange idea . . . If your life is entirely pre-determined, then why bother doing anything at all? If it is meant to happen, why bother doing anything more than you need to? To me, the belief in fate invites laziness. It invites nihilism. I groan at the idea.

German philosopher Friedrich Nietzsche popularized the idea of *"amor fati,"* a phrase that means "love of one's fate"—or even, implicitly, "love your fate." While the Hellenistic stoic philosophers never knew this phrase, they embraced the idea all the same. Any decision the individual makes is because they were fated to make it. While I have my own issues with this idea as stated above, it's by no means an idea that I think is necessarily wrong, just not one I personally adopt. This idea of loving your fate was just another way of saying love your hardships. That idea, I absolutely adore!

I could write three chapters alone on my mindset towards enduring hardships. This theme runs strongly throughout this book. As I mentioned in my redactions, I want to see your hell. I want to see where it hurts. I want this because that's when your philosophy and your religious views matter most. I want to know how you held it together, using your philosophical and/or religious glue. That's what drove me to write this book.

I've been fortunate in various ways throughout my life. I don't want to spoil the revelations, but some of the most fortunate things that have happened to me were absolute shit at the time. I was built in the same way as anyone else, from a seed and an egg. I was raised under relatively normal circumstances. But the events that occurred over the past 30 years, some of them, were a creation of hell on earth. Perhaps I'm too jaded but over time I came to really embrace the idea of loving your obstacles. So much that maybe I create them at times when I don't need to. It's something I'll continue to work on.

But once you've seen hell, and really, truly, spent some time exploring it, you also find new ways to escape. Even if you ran headfirst into that darkness, once there you figured out how to escape it. Vowing to never go back through that door.

Yet, something about that door across the hall is *exceptionally* inviting . . .

And you'll go through that one, too. But it'll be a little easier this time. And a little easier the next. Before you know it, the calm is *too* calm. The dragon reappears, almost within reach, and you feel like you can fly . . .

Stoicism has influenced my exploration of both light and dark periods of life. It played an important role in my discovery of pagan belief systems. As far as I'm concerned, the gods are there to see me through it. *With Lucifer On My Side* isn't just the title of this book, it's also the reality I have come to trust. I was given the tools I needed to navigate life, and I choose to do it in the ways that follow.

PAGANISM

How does paganism fit into all of this?

It doesn't.

Paganism itself isn't a philosophy. It's an umbrella term for various European mythological belief systems.

My ancestors are all from Italy as far back as we can date (which admittedly, isn't that far). So naturally as I began to venture into pagan studies, I started with the Romans. Though that wasn't the only reason.

My introduction to Roman paganism was born out of studying the origins of Lucifer and Satan. In *Profiling Lucifer* I explained that Lucifer was another name given to the Morning Star, which isn't a star but rather the planet Venus. The Romans worshipped the goddess Venus in the same way the Greeks venerated Aphrodite. A goddess of love, beauty, fertility, prosperity, victory and more, she was one of the most loved in the Roman religion.

This helped dive me into my Roman polytheistic studies. And I was happy I did. I found various rich traditions stemming from the belief systems and religious practices among the Roman people (ditto the Greeks).

The Greeks and Romans had their own way of exemplifying these ideas. Through festival, rituals, and tradition all of them carried forward a matching ethos. A tradition built on honor, duty, responsibility, living with purpose and intent, embracing nature in all its forms—and, as I came to find—strength.

For whatever reason, I have always admired the strong. Whether physical or mental, strength is the result of continuously applying resistance and pressure. As a result, the new form is stronger, able to endure, withstand, and withhold additional resistance and pressure.

As I continued to study the explanation of life's challenges, and how to endure them, I was reminded of a book I read when I was 19 years old called *Meditations* by Marcus Aurelius, a Roman emperor. I found this similar sense of stoicism among followers of a religion particularly alluring. From here I dove into other pagan beliefs—becoming quickly fascinated with the Nordics, as the tales of heroism among their gods came to life.

It would take multiple chapters to go over every mythology or tradition under the pagan umbrella that I find important and of great value. Instead, I am going to zoom in on the Greek myth of Prometheus:

Prometheus was a titan—a gigantic spiritual entity—who didn't oppose the head of the divine pantheon, Zeus, during the war against the titans. He stayed out of the hostilities, remaining neutral. As a result, Zeus put Prometheus and his brother Epimetheus to work gathering animals to populate the earth. Talents were distributed among animals so indiscriminately that when Prometheus made man out of clay, he realized all of the talents were already taken. When he brought his creation to the Goddess Athena, she was so impressed she breathed life into man. Still Prometheus thought man was incomplete. He wanted humanity to be separate from the other animals. Athena advised Prometheus to grant fire to man—and once so equipped, humanity quickly jumped to the top of the food chain.

Zeus decided that humankind should give praise to the gods through sacrifice. Prometheus adamantly disagreed. He tricked Zeus by killing a bull and splitting it into two separate piles. He did this so Zeus would think humanity had obediently sacrificed an animal. One pile had the good meat but looked small and was covered with animal fur. The other pile was bigger but full of nothing but bones and useless entrails. Prometheus knew Zeus would go for the bigger pile and he did.

Realizing he was tricked, Zeus decided to punish mankind by taking fire away. Struggling to maintain their status—or even live—without it, they were doomed. Prometheus daringly stole the sacred fire and gave it back to them. As man's progression began again Zeus took notice. Furious with Prometheus, Zeus punished him by chaining him to a rock. Every day a giant bird devoured his liver, causing him excruciating pain. And each day the liver regenerated only to be devoured by the bird again, so he had to suffer that pain endlessly.

Zeus offered to release Prometheus. All he had to do was take back the fire from man. Seeing as Prometheus was the patron of humanity, he declined the offer to end his own suffering for mankind. Mankind was his favorite creation and he wanted to see them flourish. He knew that wouldn't be possible without fire. This meant centuries of torture for him—until the great hero Hercules killed the bird and freed Prometheus from his chains.

Jeremy Crow, a former leader of Michael Ford's The Greater Church of Lucifer and author of various Luciferian ritual practice books, once stated in a live YouTube chat that if Prometheusism was a philosophy, it would perfectly encompass his views.

You can find parallels between the story of Prometheus and the story of Azazel. Not so much in origin, but in their role for humanity. Both entities gave humanity the tools it needed to flourish. Azazel was the leader of the Watchers, a legendary group of angels who lusted after women who duly gave birth to the Nephilim, giants that walked the earth—until God destroyed them because they were seen as an abomination. Azazel is credited for showing humanity the art of war, how to create weapons—but more importantly, just like Prometheus, how to climb the food chain.

The story of Prometheus is not unlike that of the serpent in Eden from the Gnostic view.

It's like there's a connection between these myths . . .

LUCIFERIANISM

Luciferianism is a combination of various ancient mythologies and schools of thought. From Gnosticism to Hermeticism, Theosophy to Hinduism, Buddhism to Sumerian. But if we really want to understand Luciferianism, we have to look at it through the lens of Madame Helena P. Blavatsky (HPB), the 19th-century Russian guru.

HPB is arguably the starting point from which almost all modern esoteric or occult practices come. She is the author of *Isis Unveiled* and *The Secret Doctrine*. Most would agree that at some point in her 25 "lost" years she obtained the knowledge needed to write these books. Although very little is known about this time in her life, she was known to travel across Europe and Asia, studying various forms of spiritual philosophy along the way. HPB is also the main founder of the religion *Theosophy*, a word meaning "divine wisdom."

HPB is important to Luciferianism for multiple reasons. The most important was her understanding of Lucifer. HPB didn't believe that Lucifer was the evil side of the duality of God; she saw Lucifer as the liberator, partly because she followed the Gnostic thought process which states that the God of the Old Testament (Jehovah) intended to enslave humanity. To her, as the Gnostics, Jehovah and the Demiurge become one, and Lucifer (also manifested as the serpent in the garden of Eden) was the liberator of all mankind. Not unlike the Greek myth of Prometheus, which she utilized in her book, *The Secret Doctrine*.

HPB's understanding of Lucifer was further shown in her Theosophy organizations, naming the newsletter for them nothing other than *Lucifer*. Her first issue was released in 1897 and it held an article entitled "What's in a name?" In this article, she goes into further detail as to why she chose *Lucifer* as the title. HPB explained that mistranslations have essentially polluted this exceptional title and word.

Lucifer was meant to bring the light to the darkness, not be the king of it.

The enlightened concept of Lucifer is found in some surprising places. Even in the New Testament description of Jesus!

Revelation 22:16 states;

"I, Jesus, have sent My angel to testify to you of these things for the churches. I am the root and the descendant of David, the bright morning star."

This translation was in Greek. If you take the Greek words and translate them to Latin—where the word "Lucifer" originates—it would state, "I, Jesus, am Lucifer."

Recognizing this undeniable truth, HPB found it necessary to give Jesus the title of "Lucifer," which makes sense seeing as the Bible did it roughly 1,600 years before her. Lucifer wasn't evil. Lucifer wasn't bad. Lucifer was a title for those working in accordance with the highest God. Lucifer was a title for those who had found divine wisdom—and embodied it.

Azazel (the leader of the Watchers—fallen angels who impregnated earthly women with the Nephilim) was important to HPB for the same reason the Gnostic serpent in Eden, or Prometheus, or Jesus Christ were important to her; These myths present the idea that individual entities within the world came to disrupt humanity's lowly condition by giving them the tools to rise above it towards excellence.

HPB would call these entities by their correct names. But they all earned the title of *Lucifer*.

Fast forward a little over 100 years and we can introduce a man named Michael Ford. He was the founder of The Greater Church of Lucifer and author of various Luciferian occult books. He organized the Luciferian philosophy into one unified idea, which even HPB had not.

Ford added his own flair, for better or worse. He drew extensively from Anton LaVey and his philosophy of Satanism. (The next chapter is all about the connection between LaVey's egocentric-based philosophy of Satanism and the spiritual-based philosophy of Luciferianism.) His integration of Satanism was met with some criticism. Still, he is arguably the most recognized person speaking or writing about Luciferianism today.

Ford didn't just bring Satanism into the mix. He also included the idea of the "daemon," originally inspired by the ancient Greek philosopher Socrates. A "daemon" is not another word for "demon." A daemon was a guiding spirit of sorts who Socrates said would not tell you what *to* do, but rather what *not* to do. With this introduction of the daemon to the Luciferian philosophy came a slew of ancient mythological names, mostly from *The Lesser Keys of Solomon*, a highly popularized grimoire used by those who practice ritual magic, and the Goetia.

Not dissimilar to Socrates' concept, the daemon in the Luciferian philosophy is a guardian angel of sorts. One that the Luciferian could work with through ritual—and more importantly, life—to finally embody their highest self.

Throughout the book you will see references to Lucifer, Azazel, Belial, Samael, and Lilith as entities, or gods. Because of their traditional stories, these entities are all commonly recognized in Luciferianism. All references to the names above are examples of daemons.

CHAPTER TWO

THE OBVIOUS CONNECTION BETWEEN LAVEYAN SATANISM AND LUCIFERIANISM

*"As above, so below;
As below, so above."*

—Three Initiates
The Kybalion

IT AMAZES ME THAT THIS ISN'T MORE WIDELY talked about or understood. Perhaps someone has published something about it, somewhere. Honestly, I'm not looking. To me this is enough. This is a strictly philosophical debate where both sides can be reasonably understood.

Luciferianism is a byproduct, in large part, of Gnosticism. As previously discussed, Gnosticism is an early—almost 'alternative'—Christian belief system that places God beyond human comprehension and ascribes the physical, imperfect world to the creation of the

Demiurge, a lesser god equated with the biblical Jehovah. To the Gnostics, the Demiurge is a good representation of what any kind of developed spiritual individual is supposed to reject. The Demiurge is responsible for materialism, greed, and envy. The Gnostic would work throughout his or her entire life to reject the Demiurge as it is the only want to reach the true creator God.

Kinda sounds like Buddhism, doesn't it?

Some hints of Islam, perhaps?

Oh, look! More dots to connect!

Let's ask, what drives the internal desire for the material? In part, greed and envy of your fellow man. In part, selfish desires. In part, the ego.

But we are plagued with that nasty prick, aren't we? The ego. Pft. What a disgusting thing! Surely it should be rejected and completely cast aside! It easily becomes a rejection of the Demiurge, and as a result, material or egotistical desire. Through detachment from the material world, we can reach an enlightened state, as Buddha taught us. Even the Hermeticists, who gloried in the potential of human life, practiced this rejection of the material. A sort of combined idea of lifelong minimalism.

Let's turn to Anton LaVey and his philosophy, Satanism.

Does Satanism promote a rejection of the material in an effort to obtain a heightened spiritual awakening?

Arguably, the opposite.

Instead, LaVey preached to the side of humanity that is largely dismissed and ignored by the traditional philosophy of Luciferianism—the carnal beast inside every human being.

While Luciferianism answers a great many questions about the world around us, it doesn't touch *much* on the animalistic side of humanity. The carnal beast within man, begging for release from time to time in whatever way the person might embrace. Some do this through music, some through fighting, some through meditation.

Oh yes, even meditation, and as an extension, ceremonial practice. Rituals are common among all esoteric, occult, and Left Hand

Path practices. Both the Satanist and the Luciferian exercise the beast within through this method, even if the rituals themselves look dramatically different.

Personally, this still isn't my preferred way of exorcising my inner carnal desires. I think people hear carnal and automatically think of sexuality but the term encompasses much more than that. Think of carnal as one and the same as your base animalistic desires. What's important here is that the ritual is an expression of man as an animal as opposed to an individual on a spiritual journey. The 7th Satanic Statement of The Nine Satanic Statements in *The Satanic Bible* (1969) rings true here;

> ***Satan represents man as just another animal, sometimes better, more often worse than those that walk on all fours, who, because of his "divine spiritual and intellectual development," has become the most vicious animal of all!***

What's this have to do with Luciferianism?

Nothing. That's the point.

Luciferianism is the *yang* to the Satanic *yin*. Yang representing order, life, and the masculine. Yin representing chaos, the unknown, and the feminine. Luciferianism is a philosophy of spiritual development. Those sources of divine knowledge the Gnostics believe in are hidden around the world, and to find them you must dig deep into unknown, often hidden and even unresearched, areas of life. It's not easy. Satanism, on the other hand, is fundamentally an egotistic philosophy. A much more "in-the-now" idea centered around selfish desire. The two cancel one another out.

The contradiction is obvious. LaVey promoted greed in men to satisfy their carnal wishes. "Indulgence instead of abstinence," right? LaVey took Satanism to be left up to the individual when living out their desires. To use their own judgment and reject a traditional ethos or even basic morality if they did not serve them.

For example, most of us in the western world are aware of the saying, "treat others as you want to be treated". The Satanic version of that is, "treat others the way they treat you".

Luciferianism follows the path of the divine kings who gave a moral compass to their followers along with utilizing science and reason. Even beyond that, Luciferianism strongly rejects the material and worldly desires. There's a clear rejection of the super ego and a strong, Buddhist-like influence of living detached from *things*.

Here is the obvious incompatibility between the two.

The conversation could end here. It would satisfy the Luciferians, some of whom might reject any idea that they should be associated with such a slimy philosophy. It would satisfy the Satanists who reject any idea of a cosmic being, whether described by the Hermeticists, divine kings, or "spiritual" leaders of today.

I could easily understand both ideas. But understanding an idea and agreeing with it are two separate things.

When I originally wrote *With Lucifer On My Side* I went into it with the idea that, while useful to many, rituals are not the only way you can reach a heightened level of self. The esoteric Buddhists, Luciferians, Satanists and Thelemites might all disagree, at least to some extent, but in my opinion—formulated from my own varied experiences—spiritual development can come out of the carnal just as much as it can come out of researching the occult. In my case, even more so.

If you see Satanism and its promotion of the ego as simply a tool to help you acquire the material, I suggest you widen your perspective. Quite a bit, actually.

You can't look at someone who has a successful business and automatically see them as greedy because their business turns a large profit. I think that would be pretty unfair. Just as it would be wrong to consider a commercial pilot greedy because their job pays them a large salary. Simply having the material (or access to it) doesn't mean that you are attached to it. But try to pull their jobs away from them and you'll have a battle. The business owner wants his company to grow more. For the same reason the pilot wants to maintain the status of their impressive flying record. Their success is an extension of their ego.

Now, are they complaining about their salaries? Probably not. But you know what? You wouldn't either. So get off your high horse. Living humbly is a rational, nice, enlightened idea until it becomes an option versus a necessity.

"What would you buy with a million dollars?"

Unless your answer to that question is "absolutely nothing," don't argue with me on this. You have materialistic wants (and needs) just like everyone else. And that's okay. Matter of fact, you should want more. Think bigger . . .

Both the business owner and the pilot could be Satanists or Luciferians. Or Theosophists. Or Thelemites. Because simply exercising your ego through your actions cannot be considered, by itself, solely egotistical. It's just one of the bases from which a person's actions are derived.

Would it be any different if it was someone with a successful help-the-homeless charity? The CEO of a successful charity is still making a good salary. Do we consider them egotistical because of this alone? Of course not. Even if the goal is to eradicate homelessness, the CEO will feel a sense of pride as his charity helps more and more people. His actions are rooted in his ego, but the result of those actions is undeniably selfless.

Satanism gives a realistic approach to life in the 21st century (and before) and can be used to assist a Luciferian as they direct themselves through their own journey. Moses was awfully hard-nosed at times. Jesus was calm and passive. Muhammed was headstrong. Their philosophies only sometimes reflect their state of mind as a human being. By this there was an understanding of compassion among your fellow man, in Christianity. But nowhere was the carnal discussed in any kind of bright light. It is like you had to entirely reject this side of your being. Another way of looking at it would be a rejection of your ego, long before the Freudian psychology we understand today.

I would make the argument that a single action can be both selfish and selfless at the same time. And more so, the intent can be both selfish and selfless at the same time.

Remember the Buddhist idea of compassion, "this is no longer good for me, which means it is no longer good for you. We should both cease whatever it is we are involved in so we can benefit from something else elsewhere?"

Can we not look at it from both a compassionate and selfish viewpoint? You cease your activity with another person because it is no longer in your best interest. Meaning you won't give the effort they deserve. Meaning you will be wasting their time. Their future headaches, caused by your indifference, are avoided. Isn't ceasing the activity that doesn't fully benefit them also going to benefit you? And even more so, wouldn't you become automatically aware of this selfish end of your compassion? Therefore, your intent, in this circumstance, can be equally selfish and selfless at the same time . . .

So, when we have a philosophy that glorifies the carnal side to man, even promoting indulgence instead of abstinence—or even personal discipline—it seems clear that this would directly oppose a philosophy that says to reject worldly desires.

Why can't they align? Why can't a man's carnal desires, or even his egotistic desires, coincide with a rejection of the Demiurge and be used to advance spiritually?

I have certain fitness goals that are entirely selfish. I am not a sponsored athlete. I am not a fitness influencer of any kind. I am not paid for my strength and conditioning work. It was a goal I chose because I enjoy working out. Though, I am not a hobbyist. If I am going to do something I want to be great at it. Therefore, my strength goals are an expression of my ego. My own internal and personal want to be measurably stronger than what's expected of me.

Say I achieve the two-times body weight bench press I've been training for. Will I not be able to look back on the past years of working towards this specific goal and learn a great deal about myself, as a human being? Does this not allow me to fully recognize my capabilities as an individual? Does this not give me a gnostic experience that I would not have been able to understand otherwise? Who's to say that divine knowledge can't be found on a path driven by the ego? Does this not provide me with spiritual development?

I reject the idea that divinity cannot be found in the material. Most in the western world would see a blanket as just a blanket. Few look at it and realize that it's the difference between a child surviving the cold winter on the streets, and perishing. If the child finds a blanket its purpose becomes divine. Its purpose saves a life. Whereas I have a blanket for my dog to lay on, someone else depends on that to get through life. Either way, the blanket it dead. If life ever existed in the material it is made of, it has been long gone.

Still, we can find the divinity in something that simple.

"Split wood, I am there. Lift up a rock, you will find me there."

Jesus Christ in the Gospel of Thomas. In this passage Jesus is telling Thomas divinity can be found everywhere you look. If it is in wood, an inanimate object that once held life, why would it not be in the rock as well? Did the universe not create the rock? Is it not therefore "birthed" by the same material as anything else the universe holds? Do the same rules of correspondence not apply? Does this idea not fall in line with Gnosticism? If Sophia created the material and soul, and the soul was supposed to hold the Divine Spark (resulting in the reason humans have it), why would divinity not reside in the material as well?

Meet Satanist Joe.

Joe wasn't raised to be particularly religious in his suburban American home in Arizona, though his parents at least professed that they believed in God (Christian). One day in the bookstore he wandered from the car magazines into the occult section and saw *The*

Satanic Bible. It piqued his interest and he picked it up, mesmerized by the glowing red man and symbol behind him on the back of the book.

Joe was 16 years old that day. Satanism became his philosophical home. His base. The philosophical rock he leaned on while traveling through life. He valued the Nine Satanic Statements, Eleven Satanic Rules of the Earth, and the Nine Satanic Sins. He utilized Anton LaVey's *The Satanic Rituals* to fulfill his meditative and goal-setting desires.

One of the first Satanic ideas that really caught his attention was the Nine Satanic Sins (from *The Satanic Bible*). He had found all of them to be true. Stupidity should be painful, as LaVey suggested! The people he disliked most in high school and college had the air of pretentiousness around them. Joe was unique in many ways. Eventually he came to realize this, but that also meant accepting others were not like him. Joe was well liked but a lone wolf type, never falling victim to herd conformity. Immersed in classic cars, it was where he made sure he didn't commit the 9th Satanic Sin, a lack of aesthetics.

Joe felt the Eleven Satanic Rules of the Earth (also from *The Satanic Bible*) were clear guides to live by in our modern society. He appreciated the idea of "treat others the way they treat you," opposing his family's Christian base of, "treat others as you want to be treated". The Eleven Satanic Rules of the Earth perfectly spelled that idea out. It was a series of ideals he lived by closely.

If Satan was meant to represent everything LaVey said in the Nine Satanic Statements (also from *The Satanic Bible*), as far as Joe saw it, who couldn't follow this guy!

Satan represents humanity, he thought. An idea he appreciated. Joe didn't connect with Christianity because he was against it, he just saw it as unrealistic. An outdated way of life. His approach to Abrahamic religions was similar to Friedrich Nietzsche's idea from this ideal *Ubermensch*, "pity the weak."

Joe lived in Austin, Texas as a bar manager in the downtown district. He worked in this industry for three years before he ever touched cocaine. Seeing its powerful hold over people he decided to stay away, figuring it wouldn't serve his life well. Plus, "self-preservation is highest law," as LaVey proclaimed. Joe ate relatively healthy and worked out 2-3 times per week. He stayed active in his lifestyle.

At a friend's bachelor party in Miami, Joe decided to live by another LaVeyan ideal, "indulgence instead of abstinence!" So Joe tried coke and partied the night away with his soon-to-be-doomed groom and other groomsmen.

Upon returning home and going back to work, the access to coke was unlimited. At first it was a bump or two during rush-hour. It didn't take long but he bought his first gram to get through the shift.

Oh . . . but he had a *good* reason. He didn't get much sleep the night before because he was playing video games . . .

About 10 months out from that bachelor party, Joe had become a functioning addict. He lied to himself, claiming he only used when he was at work. He used on all occasions. He told himself he could stop whenever he wanted. He had felt acute withdrawal symptoms on and off for months now but couldn't admit it to himself. Eventually his life revolved around his coke addiction.

One night he felt the full effects of his addiction. He hadn't used in two days due to finances being low. This was the withdrawal. This was his low point. He couldn't deny his addiction any more and cried over it in bed. He asked himself how he got there. He wasn't ready for the full responsibility of his pain.

The following morning he sat at his breakfast bar in brooding silence. He knew he needed more than the desire to quit. He needed to go back to his Satanic roots. He needed to reread *The Satanic Bible* and remember how these principles helped him navigate life so beautifully thus far.

Then he thought, *wait, didn't that lead me here in the first place? This idea of indulgence?*

Joe sat and thought about it. He had won county awards for his classic car rebuilds. That happened because he indulged in his hobby, working endlessly to be effective in his work. He dated smart, intelligent, beautiful women because he wasn't afraid to indulge in the carnal desires he had. He built close, genuine, real relationships with people because he indulged in them. So how could the idea work in those circumstances but be the villain here? Joe figured it couldn't, and therefore *he* was responsible for his addiction.

It was possible for him to leave it at the stag party, long before he reached withdrawal.

He remembered the importance of self-preservation and couldn't believe he let his health wither like he had. A once regular gym-goer now panted walking up stairs. He remembered LaVey's wish that stupidity was painful. Joe declared that it was, referring to the withdrawal he experienced. He no longer treated people like they treated him. They properly responded to this new, coke-addict, Joe with distain and he remained passive, only caring about his next hit. With this, his work suffered.

It wasn't easy but Joe made it a week sober. Completely clean, as he felt he needed to ensure he had nothing else to fall back on, like alcohol, which his coke addiction brought significantly more of. Then he made it two weeks. He started to feel like himself again. He started to go to the gym again.

Joe breathed a breath of fresh air as he woke up and hit his alarm. He made it to 30 days sober. He had no desire to use coke or alcohol, and thanked his copy of *The Satanic Bible*, realizing what sent him to the darkest place of his life was also responsible for helping him recover.

Meet Theosophist Angela.

Angela was a quiet but intelligent young woman entering college. She waved goodbye to her parents as they dropped her off at her New York university. She was going to major in literature, having a deep fascination for classical poems. She wished to be a college professor. She was clean cut, responsible, and smart.

Angela lived in the university dorms. Dorm neighbors were nowhere near as "clean" as she was. Within no time, Angela was

THE OBVIOUS CONNECTION... 37

introduced to marijuana and alcohol. Still, she wasn't much of an alcohol fan but she *loved* marijuana and became a regular smoker.

Friends she made introduced her to the world of electronic dance music (EDM) raves. These music parties were havens for hardcore drug use. Angela and her friends go to a rave and within an hour, Angela decides to try mushrooms for the first time.

The rave colors meshed. Everything had a flow. Angela was happy, high, and barely lucid as she danced the night away with her friends, taking the typical break along the way to give the "universal-cosmos" speech (if you've been to a rave you know the one, "we're all a universal oneness . . . Peace, love, unity, respect."). She kept the tradition. At one point someone told her, "Congratulations! You've opened your Third Eye!"

Angela had never heard this term before and remembered it into the next afternoon, when she woke up. She discovered the "Third Eye" was a Hindu concept—popularized by Helena Blavatsky, creator of the Theosophy religion—that basically states you have opened your "eye" to the spiritual world. It was a sort of expansion on a Rene Descartes idea that because the pineal gland had no other half, unlike everything else in the brain, it must be the center of one's being, or the base of their soul. (The pineal gland is responsible for producing melatonin in the brain, which regulates your sleeping schedule, and hormone levels—but its overall purpose is not yet fully known.)

(The symbol at the start of each chapter is the *Sigil of Lucifer*, taken from a 18th century grimoire called *Grimorium Verum*. It has a striking resemblance to the depiction of the pineal gland in the 1664 edition of *Treatise of Man* by the French philosopher Rene Descartes. The *Treatise of Man* was exploration of man and the soul that resides within him, searching to understand the connection between them.)

(Between Descartes' exploration of the pineal gland, the 18th century grimoire (which extensively covers chief demons and their invocation sigils in its Book One), and Blavatsky's "Third Eye" popularization, the symbol took hold.)

Angela fell in love with esoteric studies, which were always accompanied with drug use. By her sophomore year she was a full blown "love and light" drug addict. Marijuana, mushrooms, ecstasy, MDMA (Molly), K2, acid, alcohol, and the occasional opiate complemented her reckless and free-loving attitude. She swore these drugs helped her reach God. Totally convinced of their curious superpower, she continued to indulge, thinking she was creating this direct pathway to the divine, completely unaware she was driving herself further from it.

Angela's studies fell second to her new lifestyle. She didn't care. She was reaching *God*. The *God*.

"Fuck a college degree!" she once explained . . . stoned.

Angela was at a rave like any other weekend. She took drugs there from her usual connections. She danced with the same people. But this time she met a new friend. A tall, dark, and handsome senior named Corey. Angela and Corey bonded over acid trip stories and soon their friendship turned physical.

The last thing Angela remembered was kissing him at the rave.

She woke up in the hospital, surrounded by her parents who looked worried sick. Angela came to find out Corey had taken her to a secluded area and she started to feel ill. Corey wanted to continue with his physical adventures, Angela did not. She pushed him away and eventually struck him in the genitals. He kneeled over in pain before popping back up and giving her a black eye. The hit triggered the overdose that had already begun and Angela fell to the ground convulsing. Another raver saw what happened and called the cops.

She was taken to the hospital where they did a drug test on her. Multiple substances showed up on the report, including alcohol, marijuana, opiates, and cocaine. Her parents became aware of her addiction via Angela's doctors and nurses. They explained to her parents she would experience some withdrawal symptoms for weeks—and some for months. Her parents, never having any real experience with drug use, automatically assumed the worse.

To be fair, it was bad.

Angela was pulled out of school and her parents brought her home in hopes she could sober up. The first three weeks were hard but as the fourth rolled around, she felt like herself again, for the most part anyway. She decided to leave the esoteric philosophy behind her, seeing it as a gateway for the ugliest sides to life.

She saw Blavatsky's use of hash as an invitation to do so when she would talk about these ideas with equally high and uneducated friends. Using psychedelics was a natural accompaniment to those activities and before you know it, Angela and her friends became totally convinced their English professor is a Divine King because he referenced Hinduism a couple times in class.

If this doesn't make sense to you, good. It's not supposed to. High thoughts, more often than not, are non-sense and shouldn't be paid much attention to (the rare straggler, that golden high thought, is pretty uncommon. Still, if you ask people who use drugs often, I can assure you they will disagree as they tell you their *awesome* ideas that generated when they were stoned. I know, I used to be one of them.)

She went back to her university, even if on parental probation. She understood and didn't mind. Without the partying she found other activities to occupy her time. Part of which included exploring the Eastern history section of the school's library.

To her surprise, a history class was offered the next semester on Eastern history and religion. She hadn't returned to her esoteric studies but saw no harm in learning more about Buddhist and Hindu ideals.

The class had to write a thesis on Eastern studies represented in the post-Renaissance world. Angela immediately knew the topic she was going to write on . . .

She didn't go into this project with an intention to glorify Blavatsky. She wanted to destroy her. How dare she take the *anja* (or chakra responsible for the connection to the *Brahman*, the Hindu version of Hermeticism's "the ALL" or the Gnostic "Monad") and pervert it! The Hindu people greatly respected and valued their chakra system and Blavatsky came in the picture and diluted it with drugs!

Due to how she discovered esoteric philosophy, she could not separate drug use and Blavatsky. In her head, Blavatsky promoted drug use because Angela *thought* she understood it better when she was high, and therefore, that's the space you should research these ideas in.

Plus, Blavatsky smoked hash . . . openly.

Blavatsky believed there was multiple planes of material and spiritual existence. The one right above us was the *astral* plane. As Angela learned, this is where Blavatsky suggested a high will take you.

You don't need drugs to reach the astral plane (or any other). It can be accomplished as a fully conscious and sober being. As Angela learned, Blavatsky was against drug use. Her stance was that it greatly disrupted your connection to the spiritual world. It gives you an illusion that you are connected to it but it's just an illusion.

It was never Blavatsky that led Angela to drugs, it was her environment. Other people perverted Blavatsky's message and then sent that message to Angela. She had hardly investigated these topics on her own, trusting those who introduced her as proper teachers of this esoteric philosophy. None of them had it right. They allowed the drugs to do the speaking for them, explaining their mystical state, unable to realize it was nothing more than a magic trick drugs will play on you.

Angela was able to take responsibility for herself in this. She stayed clean, outside of the occasional alcoholic drink, and continued to research Blavatsky's Theosophy and Hinduism.

While her parents are to thank for her sobriety, Theosophy kept her there.

Philosophically there really isn't a connection between Satanic Joe and Theosophist Angela. Joe's experience and Angela's experience mirror each other in some ways, but philosophy isn't one of them.

They were both completely clean before they got introduced to drugs. They were both in an environment that promoted that kind of behavior. They both used a philosophy to their advantage.

But that's about it.

The point of these two stories isn't to connect them, it's to look at them individually and see how two completely different ends of philosophy can lead you to and from drugs, something that greatly hindered the advancement of both Angela and Joe.

Anton LaVey was more relaxed about drug use than his successors in the Church of Satan. As we've seen, Helena Blavatsky was against drug use, though she did partake in hash—regularly at one point—and the occasional drink. LaVey's warped Satanic ideals matched Joe's desire to use cocaine at the bachelor party. A warped, "love and light" perspective of Blavatsky's ideals was shown to Angela as she experienced life on her own.

Both philosophies played a role in their downfall but also played a role in their recovery.

That's the point.

Joe used Satanism to justify his exploration into drugs. Angela used the illusion of reaching God to justify her drug use. Joe, upon realizing his addiction, used Satanism to escape the hell he created. Angela had to become sober for her to fully appreciate philosophical ideals that brought her to extensive drug use in the first place.

Joe follows an ego-based philosophy—Satanism. Angela follows a spiritual philosophy—Theosophy. Both people had a desire to get sober. A selfish desire. Angela's parents kept a close eye on her, but she could've found drugs at home. Joe still worked with people who used, including during his withdrawal. But they were both willing to go through the experience to come out the other end healthier, sober, and thinking more clearly.

No matter how hard Joe argues against it, his soul exists. And not just *exists* but exists because it's a part of a larger source of life (or divinity). It doesn't matter how hard Angela tries to reach a sense of fullness in her life, she is still human and plagued with an ego. At times, a super-ego, as Sigmund Freud would explain.

Neither Angela nor Joe will be able to escape the side of them they so desperately try to escape. So why bother attempting? Why not embrace *both*? Using one when and where it is necessary and the same for the other?

Do you think if Joe embraced his spirituality his addiction would have gotten to the point it did? If he had the same understanding as Angela, would he not be able to see how extensive drug use blocks him from a spiritual world? And if it blocks him from a spiritual world, it will block him from his meditative and ritual goals. This interferes with his Satanic interests.

Imagine Angela discovered LaVey after properly researching Theosophy. The obvious idea here would be that she could take his "indulgence instead of abstinence" stance and further explore drugs. Or we can choose not to be so negative, and suggest she learned the importance of her carnal desires (*carnal* being her selfish desires, the ones not attached to her spirituality but rather her raw humanity). Her carnal desires, manifesting in part as her professional goals, is what has her continuing to seek higher education. Drug use, in one way or another, will affect her grades. If she embraced her carnal desires, and further, recognized her selfish desire as a part of that, she wouldn't allow something to disrupt her ambition. If she did, it would also affect her new—properly recognized—spirituality.

I see a rational, smart, coherent, and reasonable connection between Satanism and Luciferianism because I see it as *a yin-yang connection.* The two philosophies themselves don't match. It's their opposition that makes them work. Using one to support the other and vice versa. To keep the individual living up to their God-like state, as the Satanist would aspire. Or to keep the individual spiritually advanced, as the Theosophist would want.

Now, all the same, you could completely reject LaVey and Satanism but say yes, for the same reason, to Nietzsche, or the Stoics, who would be more in line with the Luciferian philosophy. I would absolutely understand this reasoning. LaVey is an acquired taste for some and a completely rejected flavor for others.

But does that necessarily make this reasoning wrong?

CHAPTER THREE

FATAL FLAWS OF THE CHURCH

*"Rather the kingdom is inside of you
and outside of you."*

—JESUS CHRIST
Gospel of Thomas

TRIBALISM IS A POWERFUL, EVER-PRESENT REALITY. We all belong to some kind of a tribe. Most of us to more than one. You have your work, industry or corporate tribe, your friends' tribe, your family tribe, your religious tribe, your sports team tribe, your national tribe, and so forth. These closely-bonded groups not only help define you as a person but also direct your life. Take people who follow Islam. Unlike Christians, who while they might also consult their religious community for advice and support, also rely on their personal inner relationship with God, Muslims rely entirely on their faith-based community for personal and religious guidance. For the people of Islamic faith, their tribe is essential to the direction of their lives.

Churches, on the other hand, serve a multitude of purposes. They run many shelters for the homeless, sick or abandoned animals, and abused women. Nearly every charitable cause is involved with a church-related, nonprofit organization. In most cases, these services are proactively good! I applaud anyone who takes time out of their day to help someone less fortunately than themselves.

My issue with organized religion—and as an extension, the church—is the long running historical bondage that is expected of its followers, in the name of a "God" almost all major religions agree is beyond human conceptual understanding. Regardless, churches have sworn throughout history they know what God wants . . .

The Roman Catholic church is the biggest Christian denomination in the world, and the oldest—all the others, such as Methodists or Baptists, eventually grew out of the big split of the Reformation over a thousand years after Catholicism got started. Because of its age and influence over the centuries, I'm focusing mostly on Christianity's first, and still largest Church. Although all religious structures are flawed. Whether it's a Jewish Temple, Islamic Mosque, or The Satanic Temple headquarters—every single one of them has found it impossible to uphold their religious morale in its entirety.

Consider this story . . . Once upon a time, the Catholics had a well-respected and well-known Franciscan friar (a preacher of sorts) by the name of Bernardino di Siena (1380–1444). Bernardino's job was to deliver the word of God to the citizens of Siena in the Tuscany area of what is now Italy. It is important to understand this was the age before the Gutenberg printing press. This means that the citizens, who mostly were illiterate anyway, could not read the Bible. Even if they could read their own language, the Bible was only printed in Latin. Part of the responsibilities of the church leaders was to learn Latin so they could read and interpret the Bible.

Here comes Bernardino di Siena. You have just put your trust in this random, church-appointed preacher to tell you what God wants from you. It is now his job to interpret the Bible for you. His way of thinking becomes your way of thinking. You trust this man because the church appoints him and you believe in the church because you believe in Jesus Christ as your lord and savior. It's his church—or so they tell you . . .

But men are flawed. And history has shown this time and time again.

Did he always preach what was in line with the church's doctrine? It's impossible to say because no one alive has ever heard his sermons directly. Though the historical sources do suggest he stuck to the official line, even though his excessive devotion to the Holy Name of Jesus—creating almost a separate cult within the church—landed him with an accusation of heresy. The silver-tongued preacher talked his way out of it, and yet Pope Martin V heaped more honors on him. He was most well-known for his stern stance against homosexuality and for rampant anti-Semitism. Even today, some claim he was the spark of the church's infamous stance against Judaism.

The Vatican facilitated when and where he would go. When he came to your community you could expect two things; first, everyone is now on their best behavior because they are being graced with the greatness that is Bernardino di Siena. Second, start the bonfires and burn some faggots because sodomy is a sin. He gained his reputation for sanctity partly by throwing gays into bonfires.

It takes absolutely nothing to point your finger and say that someone is gay. It takes nothing to look at your farming neighbor, who is also your competitor, and say to church authorities that you saw him engaging in sodomy with another man. The church rounds this person up, throws them into a fire, now you reap the benefits of killing off your competition, through the name of God—all inspired, by that saintly Bernardino.

We saw these same issues in the witch hunts in America in the 17th and 18th centuries. People who were not witches were accused of being in league with the Devil for the sole purpose of . . . who the fuck knows. Women were slaughtered by the dozens because the church said they were witches, and the church is never wrong so people believed them without question. If you do question the church, you'll be next on their hit list.

These examples are pure gold when understanding what power can do to a person or organization. When you are so brainwashed by a belief that you will do anything you can to live up to its standards, you become the enablers who allowed these actions to continue.

Bernardino in particular changed the social dynamic of Italy during the early Italian Renaissance. Nothing was worse than to be called a sodomite, a Jew, or a heretic. Having that label was a death sentence, and it all started because people were too afraid to challenge what they were being told. They were too afraid to decide for themselves what was right and what was wrong. As a result, many died, many suffered, many looked the other way as their friends, neighbors, and even close family members were killed in the name of the church or rather in the name of God.

As for Bernardino himself, well, what better way to convince someone to join your cause than to tell them if they don't, they're obviously against their God.

The Church's central organization, the Vatican, was clever. They used their influence to further the fire-and-brimstone narrative. But that isn't enough. Now that the narrative is established, the church you love and trust is going to give you an out for your sins. You are still expected to live a life in conjunction with the church and Bible, but you are also human. At some point you will sin. But alas! The Church will even help you there . . .

Just pay them.

Maybe you were raised Catholic and decided to go to confession. Catholic confession is an interesting practice. It's God's therapy session. You go in a booth, sit behind a mesh screen, describe your sins against God, and wait for the priest on the other side to absolve you and tell you what to do. You might say you were unkind to your neighbor, or stole, or looked at your dad's porno mags, and the priest will tell you to say ten Hail Marys and three Our Fathers. You leave that booth, go to a pew, say your prayers, go home, and all is forgiven. Hundreds of years ago, for a certain sum, you could buy "indulgences," or time off from the pains of the afterlife realm of Purgatory (the Catholics' not-quite-hell). The more you paid, the more time you got off "purifying" torture. You did what the church told you to do so therefore God must forgive you, right?

On a smaller scale it is still practiced today; however the church has wised up and recognized that asking for the old indulgences is not acceptable in our society. Now they just ask for prayers and drops in the money basket. During the Renaissance they would ask for anything, from priests telling people they had to "donate" cattle to the church, to paying hefty fines, often for stupidly insignificant "sins." To be fair, the Vatican did attempt at one point to curb the ridiculous penalties but the local church leaders didn't always follow suit.

"Okay, so what? Someone sins, someone has to say a prayer. What's the big issue?"

Christians do this today without thinking about it and we are accepting of it as a religious practice, myself included. But there were so many reports of how badly—and routinely—the priesthood abused this practice.

In general, people turn to religion for one of two reasons; one, they were raised that way and don't know any better, or two, they need to feel that there's something bigger than them which would explain why certain things happen. Neither of these reasons are wrong but I have an issue when someone takes advantage of that vulnerability. When an organization does it, like the Catholic Church and their indulgences, it is just as manipulative as when a single person does it. The Vatican invested and supported the idea of indulgences. The individual priests took it too far.

A church is built around its religious texts. In Christianity, that central scriptural core, from which it gains its perspective, is the

Bible—mainly the New Testament. Much of that was written hundreds of years after the death of Jesus Christ. It was remorselessly edited over the years, and other material was simply omitted because it contained inconvenient facts. References, for examples, to the true importance of Mary Magdalene, are found in abundance on the Gospels of Thomas and Philip—but you won't find them in the New Testament. They were banned. Similarly, the story of the Watchers is not found in our modern Bibles. The Church deliberately buried these major issues in an attempt to save their position and consolidate their ideals—not necessarily around what Jesus Christ wanted, but around their own agenda, schemes, and ambitions.

Essentially the New Testament was first assembled in 325 AD during the Council of Nicaea. Though no one knows for sure what really happened behind those closed doors—records of topics for discussion still exist but little on what they actually *said*. Most scholars accept that the purpose of the Council of Nicaea was to discuss the role of Christ's relationship to God the Father, not to vote on what was included in the Bible. Though they go hand-in-hand.

From what we do know, the Arian controversy was a major topic of debate. The Arians were a Christian sect who believed Christ was more divine than mere man, but no more than God the Father. Jesus Christ, being born of God, had not always existed. The other side of the argument is that Jesus Christ was the human representation of the divine. This is the side of the argument that was agreed upon. If the church decided to go the other way, Jesus is human. If Jesus is human, He isn't divine. If Jesus isn't divine, Christianity (as we know it) falls apart. This was a huge deal and set the seal for much of future Christian belief. (It was certainly a huge deal for the followers of Arianism—the council declared them heretics.)

The Roman Emperor Constantine convened the Council of Nicaea, made up of very early Church scholars. Famously, he is supposed to have had a vision of a cross and the words: "In this sign shall I conquer," which allegedly converted him to Christianity, but the jury really should still be out on that. He was born and raised pagan and I believe he died a pagan. Regardless, he loved his empire. So when he saw the hold Christianity was having on its many Roman converts I think he saw a way to keep his empire alive. It is because of this transition that some say Emperor Constantine was a Christian. I think he just saw the writing on the wall.

That empire still lives today in the Roman Catholic Church. There's simply too much pagan influence for it not to be. Emperor Constantine and his pagan influence flowed into his Council of Nicaea influence. The process of conversion among the Roman locals was gradual and for centuries the pagans and Christians lived among one another as the Romans and Jews lived among each other. Not to say the rise of Christianity didn't result in conflict—it definitely did—but it was a gradual process and the majority of battles occurred after the death of Emperor Constantine.

Follow me on the three ideas I mentioned above: Mary Magdalene being next to lead Christianity, the Gospel of Thomas, and the Watchers (Nephilim).

Mary Magdalene was a woman who is said to have walked with Jesus Christ. Some speculate that she was the wife of Jesus but there is no hard evidence. Interestingly, the very idea horrifies most priests because it shows Jesus as only too human. A Jesus who falls in love and has sex can't be divine. To compound their horror, the banned—or "Gnostic"—Gospels make it clear that Jesus regarded Mary as so important He saw her carrying on His mission after His death—virtually proclaiming her His successor. The Gnostic Gospel of Mary (Magdalene) even has her rousing the deeply depressed disciples after the crucifixion and inspiring them to spread the Gospel.

Keep in mind the position and roles of women at that time. Women were strictly meant to be seen, rarely heard. It was their job to take care of the home and bear children for men. According to the Church, Jesus's apostles were all men. At that time if a woman was seen around that many men she would be called a scarlet, perhaps contributing to the pronouncement of a much later pope that Mary Magdalene was a prostitute. So this idea that a woman, who came after other male apostles and formed a special relationship with Jesus Christ, and was destined to lead Christians as a whole is pretty insulting to the status and dynamics of society at that time. In the generations that followed, well, put yourself in their shoes; you have worked your entire life to gain your position in government or whatever it is and now there is this idea that your wife, your quiet, weak, child-bearing wife is now supposed to be on the same playing field as you? And not just your wife, but women in general? Women, who don't go to war, who don't own anything at all, who aren't educated, are now supposed to be equal?

It is important to keep in mind that while in America we like to act like there is a separation of church and state (there isn't) back then, they didn't try to hide it. The church and government were technically separate, yes, but they ruled alongside one another. In the same way that Jews and Romans worked with one another, the Romans and rising Christian base eventually worked with one another. If women are now at the same position as men in the church, that means that they will be at the same position as men in government.

Most controversial material about Mary Magdalene's relationship with Jesus is in the Gospel of Thomas. You won't hear it read in church on Sunday or even taught in seminaries. It was rejected by the church as being inauthentic because it essentially said that a centralized church was unnecessary because the Kingdom of God was everywhere.

Mostly, the church doesn't recognize the Gospel of Thomas because it is a Gnostic writing, not a mainstream Christian scripture. Gnostics were anathematized pagans though. In fact, they were a Christian movement that ran parallel with the Church of Paul and Peter but they saw the creation story differently. They also interpreted the purpose of God delivering Jesus Christ to us differently in that Jesus was meant to be a role model but not a divine being (least not in the typical Christian sense).

Remember the Arian controversy at the Council of Nicaea? Gnostics were more or less the other side of that argument.

If Jesus is human, He isn't divine. If Jesus isn't divine, Christianity falls apart. It ceases to exist in the eyes of your modern Christian. To the Gnostics Jesus was a role model for how humans should treat one another. They also believed that each individual was potentially divine, and if they came to realize that inner destiny they could see the Kingdom of God on Earth and return to Eden, or paradise on Earth.

Though this will surprise—and even shock—most modern church-goers, scholars around the globe recognize the Gospel of Thomas as the closest record that has ever been found to directly quote Jesus Christ. Regardless, the church realizes that if it accepts this record as factual or authentic then it will lead to the end of their two millennia reign. Can you imagine if the Catholic Church lost its power? If people stopped relying on the church for their spiritual inspiration and guidance for how to live a life that would be accepted by Jesus Christ?

The mayhem that would ensue would be devastating to the organization. Which, if you ask me, is pointless seeing as Jesus is pretty clear about the type of person you need to be to gain acceptance into heaven.

Next, let's look at one of my favorite biblical stories that was discarded during the Council of Nicaea; the story of the Watchers and the Book of Enoch. The Book of Enoch is another biblical canon not recognized by the largest organization within the Roman Catholic Church, the Latin Catholic Church. The Roman Catholic Church is separated into seven different branches and the largest is the Latin Catholic church. There are also certain branches of Catholics in Africa that do accept the Book of Enoch as authentic.

The story is essentially that angels—the leader of which was Azazel—left heaven to go to earth to watch and lust after women. Over time the angels started to mate with the women who duly gave birth to what were called "Nephilim"—the Watchers. God didn't like this so He banished them.

Of course the church can't have this! Can you imagine what Christians would think about heaven if angels were even trying to escape it to lust after women? All hell would break loose!

Heaven forbid.

We have two books, the Gospel of Thomas (and other Gnostic scripture) and the Book of Enoch, and the Roman Catholic Church accepts neither. If either or both were accepted as true and authentic, the Roman Catholic Church would cease to flourish. Their values would be rearranged and their belief structure would no longer hold weight.

Let's fast forward.

You didn't honestly think I was going to skip over the Catholic Church's involvement in protecting child molesters, did you?

Give me some credit here.

In 2015 a major Hollywood film came out called *Spotlight*. This movie highlighted the abuse from the Catholic Church in the Boston area, but it also highlighted the fact that 6 percent of the priests in the entire Catholic Church were sexually abusing minors. This is no more than the general public but the issue here isn't so much that it happened, it is how the churches responded.

An organization like that is intended to be the pinnacle of righteousness. They are supposed to be the best that the world has to offer in terms of morality and ethics. They aren't. They are really nothing more than a brand that has to protect its public image and corporate brand. And they did just that when they knew, for a fact, that their priests were touching young children. Instead of throwing the abusers in jail, or off a bridge, they simply moved them from parish to parish in the hope that it wouldn't happen again.

This wasn't an issue exclusive to Boston, this was an issue that covered the globe. How some people woke up one morning, saw the news coverage of this story and the other stories that followed, and still went to church that following Sunday is totally beyond me.

How can some people support an organization that is proven to be that unethical, that warped—and that dangerous? How can you go and ask for guidance from someone who may have had a hand in helping a pedophile escape prosecution or may even be a pedophile themselves? How is your faith so strong that you cannot abandon the very structures that supported people who hurt children—most of whom were under 13 years old—like that? Perhaps much of this sick sexuality arises from institutional frustrations and warped thinking about human relationships.

Catholics who choose the religious life are not allowed natural human emotions and sexual practices because they are expected to be married to God, in a sense.

It is a shame that Catholic priests cannot have the same freedoms as rabbis. The simple ability of being able to have sexual contact with another human is what separates the two and the inability of the Catholic Church to understand that human contact is a need, not a want, makes no sense. It's like air, or food, or water. We crave it and we need it. This doesn't mean that there are no truly celibate priests. I'm sure there are thousands of them. But imagine how much easier it would be for priests to adhere to their lifestyles if they were simply allowed to have kids? To engage in that form of love? The Bible is against sex outside of marriage. The Bible is against sex without the intent of having children. But even the Bible doesn't say that sex should be stopped entirely.

Jews may not have the issues of their rabbis fucking children but that doesn't mean that they are exempt from flaws. They are just flawed in a different way.

Jewish culture supports total religious communal commitment. They stick within their communities on almost a commune-like level. Jews are told to be as active as they can be within their religious groups. Granted there are Reformed and Orthodox Jews and while they follow the same religion, their lifestyles are vastly different. For the purpose of this chapter, I will focus on Orthodox Jews.

The purpose of the Jewish Torah—their scripture and traditional teachings—is to create a place where only men of God exist. That is, their specific sort of men of God. Isn't this the downfall of all religions? People can't learn to share, saying we only want to be with our tribe, and before you know it you are being forced to join it or be killed for not being raised to call God Yahweh, or Jesus, or Allah. When you have a society of people who actually believe that humanity is 6,000-something years old, and nothing existed before God put it into play, the end result is going to be a closed-off religious sect who thinks their way is the only way.

It is because of their lifestyle, their temple, and their community that they are the way they are. Reformed Jews live among the rest of society and intermingle with people outside of the Jewish faith. So do Orthodox Jews to some extent, but spending too much time outside of their religious communities is usually disapproved of. Why would they want to be in a bar drinking with atheists and Christians when they could study the Torah and discuss its teachings among others who live the same lifestyle and have the same religious and world views? How is their elitist mindset any different from other elitist groups?

Orthodox Jews keep to their kind because of religious beliefs and similar backgrounds. They marry within their religion. They do not think highly of Reformed Jews who marry non-Jews. The Prime Minister of Israel called it a "Jewish Holocaust."

I hold Jewish people to the same standard as anyone else. Orthodox Jews don't care if you, an atheist, Christian, Muslim, or whatever marry outside of your faith, but it isn't acceptable for them. Just as a neo-Nazi doesn't care if you, a black, Hispanic, Asian, or whatever nonwhite race, marries or engages with people outside of your race, but it isn't acceptable for them.

It's the elitist mind-set that springs from religious conviction—the eternal struggle between Them and Us, our tribe and their tribe.

This brings us to our last major religious group, Muslims.

As I mentioned earlier in the chapter Muslims do not believe in a personal relationship with God, or Allah. Their prophet, Muhammad, was revealed the Quran over the course of roughly 23 years. He then spread the word of God through his religious texts.

Muslims basically believe that Allah is outside of the conception of humanity and is too distant for humans to understand. Because of this they do not seek out a personalized interpretation of his word or guidance. They simply obey his word as told to them by Muhammad. No other way. You live exactly as Muhammad says and to do anything else is punishable by death. This is also the issue of Sharia Law, which is basically state law that follows the word of the Quran.

Muslims believe that to live a life outside of what Muhammed has laid out for humanity is a horrible offense to Allah. This is why they see us as infidels. An infidel to them is a nonbeliever, but in Sharia Law there is no place for any sort of free-living Westernized society. It depends on how far the community wants to take this offense. Do they simply sit in their mosque and have their leaders teach their communities about the consequences of disobeying the Quran? Or do they want to directly follow the Quran and kill the infidel? And if you don't think that the Quran actually says that you're an idiot. It's not a particularly long religious text. You're welcome to fact-check me.

How do we recognize a jihadist? Do you think they walk around telling people that they are at war with western society? Doesn't it make more sense they would act in private and on their own, possibly even from their religious leaders at their mosque?

Many Muslims are just preaching to live a peaceful life, one that Allah would be proud of (make no mistake, the Quran promotes that too). But many are saying something else entirely. It is this small minority that supports an absolute Sharia Law—a law most westerners cannot even begin to understand what it would be like to live under. The idea of the "silent majority" in this context is irrelevant, as Brigitte Gabriel famously articulated. Millions of peaceful Muslims don't make the minority jihadists any less of a threat. This religious organization, who accepts that Allah is outside of human comprehension, is so *absolutely* sure what he wants.

Remember . . . it only takes one drop of poison to contaminate a cup of water.

Due to their notoriety I will share my views on The Satanic Temple (TST).

The Satanic Temple is an organization that uses the edgy term, "Satanism," to push their political agenda. If this organization got anything from Anton LaVey and The Church of Satan it was the theatrics of it all. They use graphic theatrics and scary-looking symbolism to get their point across.

They have seen some success, including being a force to change political law regarding abortion, religious imagery in association with state monuments, and LGBTQ laws. They are undoubtedly effective in the way they get their point across and they definitely catch the attention of the press. But that doesn't make them any less of a fool's organization. TST making political statements under the guise of a church is no different than any other church getting involved in politics. Both are wrong, but be consistent in your stance and argument.

Is integrity too much to ask for—even in, or especially in, Satanism?

Let's face it . . . Christianity and Judaism have had a strong presence in shaping America. We have "In God We Trust" on our money and the words "Under God" in our Pledge of Allegiance for a reason I'm aware of the whole separation from Communism reality but Judeo-Christian values were still strongly represented in government before that took place). I look at it from a historical point of view and therefore think attempting to change this is a waste of time and energy. When a Ten Commandments monument is at your state's courthouse, recognize it is there because it had an actual role to play in building the United States of America.

To my knowledge, TST hasn't taken on American currency or the Pledge of Allegiance, yet, but I also don't think they or anyone else should. We have the right to religious freedom and that should be enough. But to try to deny that Christianity or Judaism isn't the most common religion in our country is ridiculous and because of this fact, why try to change their mark on our society? In current forms of practice, both religions are mostly morally just and I think the vast majority of people in Western civilizations would agree.

Of course America is a nation that supports a separation of church and state (in theory). But allow me to put it like this: if you have a charity organization for the homeless and on the national board you have ten people, all Christian, do you think it is fair to suggest that their ethical, moral, and charitable codes are going to be influenced by the religion and philosophy they follow?

Of course it is! The Founding Fathers are no different. So while America is a secular nation, it was founded by God-fearing individuals whose moral and ethical compass mostly pointed to the crucifix, which undoubtedly bled into shaping the nation. Yes, America is secular, but the people who built it were not.

This is why I don't have an issue with the Ten Commandments monument being erected at a state capitol. The Ten Commandments are the most recognizable tenets of Judaism and Christianity. Those same tenets influenced the Founding Fathers. That influence flowed into federal and state law.

All the same, I don't care if it isn't erected. Nor do I care if Muslims, Hindus, Satanists, whoever else wants to have their own religious monument. The purpose of The Satanic Temple, in this regard, is to say if you open the door to Christianity you open the door to Satanism. I agree with that statement. But it is important to note that modern Satanism wasn't defined until 1966. So Satanism had no role in shaping the nation.

On the other hand, I got a good laugh out of their Baphomet stunt. It was an enjoyable middle-finger representation to Arkansas State Senator Rapert and those like him.

It's not that I am antiabortion because I'm not. I'm pro-choice. It's not that I am antiseparation of church and state because I'm not. I think there should be as much of a separation as possible. It's not that I am anti-LGBTQ because I'm not. Who someone chooses to love is none of my concern. But to use a "church" to push your political agenda is wrong, regardless of the religion that is doing it. To morph the tenets of LaVeyan Satanism into something it was not just to get that point across is disgusting. Most of all, to deny that LaVey didn't have any importance to Satanism, an argument many in that organization have made, is ridiculous. Lucien Greaves prefers to use John Milton's *Paradise Lost* as his basis of understanding Satanism as opposed to Anton LaVey's *The Satanic Bible*. In my opinion, it cheapens the religious structure that was built before he was born.

I will admit that the expulsion of Jex Blackmore (former TST national spokesman) does make them an easier pill for me to swallow. On a personal level I adamantly disagree with people like her. She tried to use her platform within TST to push a radical feminist and seemingly antifa agenda. This campaign for radical thought within TST is going to make it look like a social justice warrior organization versus a religious one. I have read the Seven Fundamental Tenets set forth by TST. I agree with them. Yet I radically disagree with Jex and her agenda. So when TST is pushing a political agenda versus a religious one, one that is open to all people who agree with those seven tenets, you can understand my confusion as to what they are really trying to accomplish.

One could argue LaVey did the same with the Church of Satan, saying it was his response to the growing counter-culture in the late 1960s. Drawing the parallel between the Church of Satan and The Satanic Temple is loosely tied together because the Church of Satan simply exists. Of course LaVey spoke openly and publicly about what it was and what it entailed but he didn't use the Church as a means to push his own agenda to the masses. That's what separates them.

The Church of Satan doesn't really do anything. To become a member you pay a $250 fee and get a red card in the mail with your name on it next to the Church of Satan logo. But the Church of Satan simply exists. They aren't in the media trying to push any kind of agenda. They fade into the background, where they've remained for the past 20–30 years. Only their members keep up with whatever is going on in that organization, which to my understanding is a celebration of different Satanic artists and imagery and the occasional Satanic Ritual that they will host. Neither of which I have any issue with.

CHAPTER FOUR

RESPONSIBILITY AND STRUGGLE

"You have the power within you to endure anything, for your mere opinion can render it tolerable, perhaps even acceptable, by regarding it as an opportunity for enlightenment or a matter of duty."

—Marcus Aurelius
Meditations

STOICS STRUGGLING CAN BE AN INTERESTING case study in what to do when the world throws obstacles in your way. If you are holding true to Aurelius, you recognize you only can control yourself. You have no control over outside events and the sooner you come to accept this, the better off you'll be. As a siderail to this point, that means you need to take full accountability for yourself. You cannot accept that you have no control over outside events, only yourself, and dismiss taking responsibility for your actions.

This could also be a bleeding-through effect of LaVeyan Satanism as one of his Satanic tenets is not to complain about anything you subject yourself to. All the same it applies to both ideals. If I believe in LaVey's idea that we should not complain about anything we subject ourselves to, and if I believe as a stoic that I have to take responsibility for all of my actions, both ideas will go hand-in-hand.

The only place these conflicts is when I have to separate taking responsibility and taking fault.

My self-defense coach taught me an interesting saying—

There are no victims—only volunteers.

If you can accept a mind-set where you take responsibility for all of your actions, that saying makes a lot of sense. I will agree there are some exceptions to that rule, but in so many other cases, there isn't.

When I was 16 or so I got my truck doors smashed in by a Ford Explorer, driven by a guy named Mark who was trying to kill me and my two passengers.

This glorious night all started off with my friend John and me trying to get drugs. We were going to get high on coke and come down with painkillers. My usual guy was dry so I had to go through someone else. That someone else was Travis. He was a real sack of shit who I had only met once before and did not like in any way but when you are dealing with drug dealers, you learn to bend on the type of people you like to do business with. For example, if I went into a pizza shop and asked for a large cheese and pepperoni and the person at the front counter gave me an outrageous price and an attitude, I would happily tell that person to eat a bowl of dick—and go to the next pizza shop. But with drug dealers, you just kind of shrug and hope it is the same quality as last time.

John and I go to Travis's house to get our goodie bags. We find out he is dry, and we have to go somewhere else to get it. Every person who buys dope is aware that is step one of a domino effect of stupid decisions. Every person who buys dope is also smiling right now because they have been there too. When you are determined to get high nothing stands in your path. If there's a will there's a way.

John, Travis, and I all ride out to the middle of nowhere to meet up with Mark. We drop Travis off at Mark's place and go park at a gas station down the street. This is step two of the stupid decision domino effect. John assured me he has known Travis his entire life, Travis would never rob him, etc. I say okay because I am determined to get high and to be fair, when I jump through hoops to get it I tend to appreciate it a bit more.

John and I sat there for a fucking hour waiting to hear from this jackass. Finally, Travis calls John and frantically tells him he will be at the gas station in a minute.

"Whoa, dude, what's wrong?" John asked.

Click.

"Oh shit. Something's wrong." John said to me as I grinned.

"Of course there is."

Shortly after Travis hung up a red Ford Explorer comes alongside. Travis opens the door and throws me the money. I think to myself *hmm, maybe this guy is okay.*

Travis and Mark are bitching at each other. It's immediately obvious that Mark is high. Travis gets in my truck and tells me to drive off. As I do, Mark is right behind me. I speed up and Mark hits the back of my truck. His Ford stalls. When I stopped, Travis opened the door to get out. The Ford magically started worked again. John and I watched this Ford Explorer with a very intoxicated driver try to run down Travis for a good two minutes. Travis was essentially running in circles to get out of the path of Mark, who was immensely insistent that Travis needed to get hit by his truck. I was parked on a side street with John watching all of this happen in a big field. There wasn't really anything I could do. If I tried to slam Mark's truck I could've hit Travis. And truthfully I didn't give a fuck about the guy so let him get hit.

Travis runs to my truck and jumps in the bed. Mark drives alongside me and slams on his brakes, turning his truck right at me. No sooner had I put my truck in drive so did Mark, and he was coming right at me.

"DUDE, COME ON! GET OVER HERE!" John yelled at me from the passenger's seat.

I didn't have time to head off so I leaned over onto the passenger side from the driver's seat. Instantly I was slammed into by Mark, who then zoomed off, burning rubber. This all happened in a matter of five seconds, from the time Travis jumped in the bed of my truck to the time Mark hit me and drove off. Fortunately, no one was hurt. My truck, while surprisingly not totaled, was in a state of absolute FUBAR. Both doors on my Chevy Silverado 1500 were smashed in. Mark's collision made my truck skid about five feet sideways. I was pretty shaken but within five minutes I found out what happened and was able to laugh about the state of my truck. Sometimes, when you're in a shit situation, all you can do is laugh.

When the cops showed up it was obvious that this was drug related. None of our stories entirely matched up. The cop who took my report found my copy of *The Satanic Bible* and gave me a lovely 30-minute speech on how and why I was headed down the wrong path, needed to turn to Jesus, etc. Of course nothing came out of this, no one was arrested, including Mark, whose information was given to the police by Travis. Called some other friends to pick me up. Went home and got a pretty serious verbal lashing from my mom. Relatively normal night for my teenage years. Minus the attempted murder.

Obviously my truck getting smashed into was my responsibility. I bent the truth by about 6,000 percent to my mom but at no point in all of that did I ever blame it on anyone but myself. Even Travis, who only furthered my hatred for him, was not at fault. I didn't have to buy drugs that night. I didn't have to keep trying when I found out my guy was dry. I didn't have to go through Travis and then Mark. I didn't have to get my truck slammed into. It was an impulsive decision that I had to deal with because it happened to me and could have easily been avoided. I was not a victim in this situation. I volunteered for the events that took place that night.

It's not always easy though, taking responsibility for everything. Sometimes you are just trying to better yourself, you have the best intentions, but something awful comes from it.

When I was 14 years old I joined my high school wrestling team. I was moved by Kyle Maynard's book *No Excuses* and figured it was my turn to try athletics (my brother was a football and track star). I don't remember if it was during a work out, practice, or match but I seriously damaged my right shoulder. To this day it still hurts from time to time.

When I was 19 years old I severely damaged my left shoulder. On average, I have been working out 2–4 times per week since I was 14 years old. I really enjoy weight lifting. It is a great stress reliever, a great work out, and hitting weight lifting goals is one of the best feelings in the world. It is a phenomenal confidence booster. You can't lie in weight lifting. You can't cheat lifting more weight. Either you follow a program, get stronger, or you don't, and stay the same or weaken.

I joined a new gym at that time and was going five days a week for an hour each visit.

I'm at the gym and decide I'm going to hit my shoulders and go to the shoulder press machine. Three sets of 10 reps at 110 lb. Increase by 10 lb. each set. At the very least I *must* hit eight reps. I transfer from my wheelchair to the machine and pump out the first set. It was hard. I decide I am only going to go up 5 lb. Second set. Goddamn, this is *really* hard. Go up another 5 lb. I make it to about five or six reps and feel an intense, sharp, crippling pain in my left shoulder. My arms drop, so does the weight. It crashes loudly but I am in far too much pain to care. I was holding my shoulder and on the verge of tears. Something went wrong.

I didn't return for about two weeks. In those two weeks my left arm and shoulder were almost entirely unusable, making my mobility nearly impossible as I need my arms to push my chair. I never went to a doctor but I definitely should have.

Again, this was my responsibility. I, like most uneducated gym goers, thought that it was all about lifting heavy. "If you lift less than 80 percent of your ability, you're wasting your time." That was my mind-set even up to last year. Now I see the benefits of lifting lighter weights, but then I didn't, and I should have been more educated. I should have had someone spot me. I should have lowered the weight after the first set. I didn't and now I have to live with the consequences.

Sometimes taking responsibility for yourself comes in the form of a harsh reality check from the Divine.

Whether it's because I fit into this mold or simply because of the fuckboy stamp I proudly wore in my 20's, I have a thing for novelty sex. I like weird. So much so that (especially after my neo-Nazi days, which we'll get to later) I tried to experience every type of woman I could. Black, Hispanic, Asian, tall, short, bigger, petite, trans, whatever. The one I never got to experience was a little person.

She was the mythical dragon, and I was the idiot chasing.

You can imagine my excitement, just two short months after a bad breakup, when my phone dinged with a match.

I had her.

Oh my God, here she is! Mi amore . . .

We spoke and come to find out, we were close in height. My prosthetics putting me a short eight inches taller than her 3'10". She wasn't attractive by any other means. Looks wise, she clearly got her aesthetics from Trailer Park Weekly with a personality that mixed white trash with a Disney adult.

I didn't care. My strawberry short cake had arrived.

We scheduled a date for the next day. It was about 30 miles from me and we were going to get lunch at some spot I never heard of. I was ready. Dressed for sexy success, freshly shaved head and lined up my beard, I was ready to meet my new conquest.

I showed up about 10 minutes early and sent her a text I had arrived. I waited about 20 minutes in my car. I restarted my phone, thinking there was clearly an issue with the hardware.

Why aren't her texts coming in? I thought. *She sent me a video confirming it was her. I know I wasn't catfished . . .*

My phone was on. I figured it takes a second for messages to arrive. Couple minutes later, I decided to call. Went straight to voicemail. I text her again. Nothing. Called again. Nothing. I sat in this fucking parking lot for 30 minutes.

I had weight training the next day and went in with puffy eyes. My trainer, who I've worked with for seven years at this point, asked me what was wrong. I explained to him the story.

"I got stood up by a midget."

He hasn't recovered from laughing, still on the floor by the bench. He's become a mascot.

The accountability here is clear. Maybe the Divine was speaking to me, trying to enlighten me to an evaluated status. Something higher than that lowly place. Above the immature and cheap desires of man.

Stop being an asshole.

I know I deserved it but my heart still breaks. The hunt for my smooshed boo continues.

Earlier I mentioned sometimes I have to separate taking responsibility and taking fault. Saying something is your responsibility and saying something is your fault is only the same when it comes from a place of your actions. Sometimes things just happen to us. I cannot illustrate this point better than through my amputation story.

By the time I was 11 my parents were going through their divorce. My mom kept that house that we moved into from Michigan and my dad went off to live in various apartments in town. One of those apartments was a shithole that he started to see go downhill. He decided to move, which my sister and I hated because we had so many friends in that neighborhood. He found a much nicer apartment complex that was significantly closer to my mom's house.

From this point until I woke up in the hospital is a blur. A lot of what follows is what my sister, parents, and people who saw it happen told me later.

I guess the day we moved my sister was annoying me. I was trying to hide from chores in my bedroom and she was being a good daughter and cleaning up. When she started the vacuum I decided enough was enough, I am going to bribe her so she won't annoy me anymore.

"You're driving me crazy! I have twenty bucks to buy us candy, let's go to the store."

"Okay."

We start heading out. My dad's new place, at that time, was in a heavy construction zone. They were widening the street he lived off and building a new intersection. Because of this the sidewalks were nonexistent, so my sister and I decided to go through the cars. The light had just turned red so traffic was slowing down.

She gets to the median, yells for me to hurry up, and I start crossing . . .

I was blindsided by a 10-wheeler dump truck. It dragged me some 30–70 feet and eventually stopped with me pinned underneath. I can still remember brief flashes of consciousness while under that truck.

I stayed under it for a while. This happened around 4:00 p.m. in a construction zone so the ambulance and all that took a minute to get there with rush-hour traffic. The police considered moving the truck but ultimately decided that it wasn't a smart idea. If the truck had moved, I would have bled out and died.

From the crash site I was taken in an ambulance to a local A&E. From there I was airlifted to a hospital about two hours away.

I was coming in and out of consciousness in the ICU. I'm still remembering today some of the drug-induced images that came to my 11-year-old mind. (The writing for this book was on the wall with what I saw—imagine an incredibly morbid Looney Toons.) I kept trying to look under the covers over my legs, so they tied my hands to the side rail of the hospital bed. I still got out of them five times. I remember my dad laughing about it before he really put some strength into tightening the knot. It worked. I couldn't get it undone after that. He won that battle.

I don't remember the first six or seven days I was in the ICU. I was in a drug-induced coma and they didn't know if I was going to make it. I don't remember my mom and the doctor telling me they had to take my legs, nor do I remember asking the follow-up questions, like "Will I use a wheelchair?" My dad and I talked about it separately but I couldn't tell you what was said.

The first clear memory I have is being moved out of the ICU into a normal hospital room. I remember seeing my dad and my mom's boyfriend at the time and being surprised because they absolutely hated one another. Seeing them in the same room and not trying to rip each other's throats out was strange to me.

I just remember knowing I didn't have legs. Kind of hard to explain: I didn't have legs anymore and that was just the way it was.

I was in the hospital for three months. I remember a lot of it though I wish I didn't. I was always a sort of loner kid. I liked to do things on my own. Anyone who has had an extended stay in the hospital knows there is zero time for being alone.

My parents wouldn't fuck off because they were so worried about me. The nurses wouldn't fuck off because it is their job not to. The doctors wouldn't stop hurting me for whatever reason. I couldn't eat for days at a time because of all of the drugs I was on. I could shit for weeks at a time for the same reason. I had to lie on my stomach for two weeks straight so my back could heal from the skin grafts. Then I had to lie on my back for two weeks so my sides could heal from skin grafts. The priest was annoying because by this time I was just pissed off and depressed about the whole situation. The last thing I wanted to hear about was Jesus and why His plan included a shorter me. Any family that came and saw me was constantly crying and making the situation extremely awkward. People that I would talk to wouldn't stop asking me about my amputations. I was meeting a lot of amputees, who were super nice people, but I didn't want to. I didn't see my amputation as my entire identity and everyone else seemed to very much disagree with that.

And the staring. People would not stop staring at me. That took years to get over.

Perhaps I'm being too negative. There were some good memories. My mom used to read Harry Potter books to me. It was nice. She spoke with a diction unmatched by my dad. My dad read those books like they were a vacuum instruction manual. Someway, somehow, he found a way to take the magic out of the Wizarding World of Harry Potter.

Sorry old man, Mom won that one every time.

He made up for it with supplying me with food. Poor guy. I was on so much medication I had zero appetite most of the time. When my appetite came, I hid it to avoid hospital food. He'd bring me take-out from wherever for me to take three bites out of a main dish and appetizer. This happened for months and I only remember him saying something about it once.

And then, Player Henry made his appearance. The finalists of American Idol Season Two came to the hospital for some PR thing. They visited us in the children's play room. I was rolled in there in a hospital bed instead of a wheelchair because I was healing from my skin grafts on my side. All of them were making their rounds and several came up to me. Upon meeting Kimberly Caldwell, I fell in love. By this point I had already discovered an appreciation for the opposite sex, and she was Venus incarnate to me.

Decided to shoot my shot and you better believe I got the number!

Only person who followed up with her was my mom.

My mom stole my opportunity to build a future with Kim Caldwell.

And she wonders where my teenage angst came from.

They once needed me to take a bath so they could change my skin graft bandages. They were scabbed on so they had to be soaked off. This was about a 20-minute process. They gave me my CD player with my KoRn CD in it. This was one of the calmer memories I have about my time in the hospital. I was able to just relax, tune everything out, and listen to *Freak On A Leash*.

But that's balanced by the horrible memory of them still having to rip those bandages off a fresh wound. Which hurt. A lot.

I think it's fair to suggest this experience introduced me to the idea of "embrace the suck." Those bandages had to be changed, whether I wanted them to or not. To do that they had to be ripped off. It had to be done. Get it over with.

I vividly remember showering at my dad's house a couple months after I got out of the hospital. It took my back two years to fully heal from the skin graphs and once again, bandages had to be changed. There was this small piece of gauze on my right side that was stuck via dried scabs. My dad cautiously tried to remove it. Little bit of hot water, small pull, repeat. This constant tugging was painful and annoying. I told him to rip it off. He said he didn't want to. I told him to get it over and rip the bandage off. He put his head down, I grabbed the sides of the shower chair, and the bandage was torn off my back, taking a thick and bloody scab with it.

I remember it hurt. But I also remember that within two minutes the pain had subsided and I was able to go back to playing video games.

Point being, if something shitty needs to happen, just get it over with. Just power through it. My amputations taught this lesson.

So, do I take responsibility for what happened to me? Yes. I made the conscious decision to cross the street that day. When crossing the street, even in ideal circumstances, a truck can still hit you. Is it my fault? No. Sometimes things just happen to you. Nothing you can do about it. Shit happens. That has been pretty much my attitude ever since. Of course I went through my "why me?" stage but as far as I remember, it was pretty short-lived. I had to look on the bright side.

I still had my arms, which I have never appreciated more. I could still have kids one day. I could still listen to heavy metal. I could still hang out with my friends. I couldn't climb a rock anymore. Not that big a deal, you know?

I always saw it as more important to realize how I reacted to this situation. At the time, I probably did a shit job but hey, who wouldn't? The amputations brought puberty on suddenly. I was freshly legless, going through puberty, dealing with my doctor's appointments, lawyers, my parents' divorce, and still trying to live a normal life. It was a lot to take on. I typically roll my eyes when people say this but I had to grow up fast. A large part of my childhood was taken from me. I had to mature quicker than my peers because I didn't have any other option. I had to do adult tasks that a 12-year-old (I turned 12 in the hospital) shouldn't have to deal with.

But hey, *shit happens*.

My biggest goal in regards to my amputations isn't so much to take responsibility for what happened. I've already done that. It is to not allow my amputations to define me. My greatest accomplishment has always been that others don't see my struggle. It's mine. Not theirs. I refuse to be a burden to anyone and a large part of that comes from gaining independence as a man and as an amputee.

Yes, at first and for many years to follow I had this giant chip on my shoulder. Who wouldn't? The idea of not being a burden was born out of that mindset. It drove me to my independence. Though now that I've arrived and been here for many years, my mindset has changed. I still see my struggle as my struggle. Therefore it is my responsibility. I think it would be distasteful to unload this on anyone else. They clearly learned how to look both ways while I stubbornly and arrogantly charged ahead into traffic.

Point being, people's personal issues should be handled by the person with the issue, not the people around them. I still hold that stance today even if I think the chip on my shoulder has been *long* smoothed out.

I still struggle with certain things today, even though it is over 21 years later. Sometimes things take a bit longer to do than they would for an able-bodied person. Sometimes I have to think about repairing my wheelchair or adjusting my prosthetics. Before I travel anywhere I have to consider if it is accessible or not, and if not, how inaccessible it is. At the end of the day I have a beautiful life filled with amazing individuals who I know see me as a person and not just as this guy without legs. While I understand the outside perspective is outside of my control, I still hold some responsibility for their view of me.

CHAPTER FIVE

DRUGS

"I don't like the drugs but the drugs like me."

—Marilyn Manson

IN THE FIRST TWO VERSIONS OF THIS BOOK, this is the part where I detail an opiate withdrawal. In 2017, I went through eight three-day detoxes alone. Not including the other withdrawals I experienced. It was miserable. Absolutely dog shit miserable. Those in the rehabilitation community have a saying: *Opiate withdrawal won't kill you, but it will make you wish you were dead.*

How accurate this is.

I no longer see the point in including that in this book. It was about 2,000 words of the most depressing and negative shit you could possibly read so I'll just sum it up for you:

Every thought you have becomes distorted. Every great memory is twisted into a negative one. Every sense of confidence is expelled. Everything you like and appreciate melts away in a disgusting pool of messy emotional dysregulation. Your body feels like the skin is peeling off, undeniable due to the crawling bugs that reside under your flesh. Your muscles could swear you just did a marathon. And in a beautiful amputee addition, welcome back the phantom limb pain sensations you hadn't dealt with for several years.

It sucked. Entirely. Fully. Terribly. Every part of it.

My drug of choice was oxycodone in the first part of 2017. Then the doctors did me the grand favor of switching to methadone. If you don't know, methadone isn't like normal opiates. It has a specific way it time-releases in your body, causing the effects to last an extremely prolonged period of time over the other opiate options like oxycodone. I'm not lying in the least when I say I didn't feel the effects fully wear off for a solid year from my last withdrawal in January 2018. That's how long it took for the brain fog to lift entirely.

These days, I keep to my marijuana and alcohol. Moderation for both. The older I got the more I appreciated psychedelics. As a younger man they never really interested me. Now, magic mushrooms and doctor-prescribed ketamine treatments do wonders for my mental health. Neither is done more than once every three months. I dabbled with microdosing shrooms and found it helpful, but like all forms of wellness, it's all-encompassing.

It has been many years since I touched the hard stuff. I don't *typically* miss it. Do I get a wild hair in my ass from time to time? Yes. On rare occasion, for no reason at all, I will crave opiates or blow. I just recognize there's nothing left for me in those substances. They were a regular part of my life since age 11 (coke started at 16). I've explored each of them in their entirety. I've lived in that space. I don't want it anymore.

All those drugs do is take you to places the Divine is rarely found.

With regards to drugs and the Divine, I did not always think that they deterred you. At one point I was certain that drugs brought you closer to the Divine. Sounds awfully hippy-ish, I know, but it's true. I used to purposely use blow because I felt it brought me closer to my daemons and their messages for me.

I made my impulsive decision to go back to college when I finished about a quarter ounce of blow in a night. I was as high as I could be but I was absolutely certain that I needed to go back to college. Every sign in the world pointed that way.

When I was 18 I moved to Fort Lauderdale to go to the Art Institute. I wanted to work on video games as a character designer. I took three graphic arts classes in high school and really enjoyed them. Looking back, the writing was on the wall. I was a terrible graphic artist. I have no idea how I passed those classes, including the college-level course. I had this false sense of accomplishment based on my proposed "good" graphic work and thought that qualified me as a skillful enough artist to get into art school.

To get into the Art Institute I had to submit a portfolio that would be reviewed by the course directors. If I am a shit graphic artist, I am an even worse illustrative artist. I forged my portfolio. At the time I had a friend who was an amazing artist. She very willingly agreed to draw my portfolio for me. I assured her I would learn more the longer I was in college to justify this moronic move. She didn't care. By doing this she was able to see for herself if she was good enough to get into art school. She was. Easily. What I didn't think about was that now her level of artistry was expected of me. Not my most forward-thinking moment.

So I turned 18, three weeks later I moved, and a couple weeks after that I started taking classes.

I had never been more discouraged in my life. My classmates were by far some of the most autistic and socially awkward people I have ever met. It was like straight out of the movie *Grandma's Boy*, a bunch of ridiculously gauche people brought together by a love of video games. Most discouraging, though, it quickly became clear to me that none of them had forged their portfolio. These kids were amazing artists, which was good because they needed something to make up for their awkward personalities. My teachers were mostly cool. I still had hope but it didn't last long.

I was now friendless in a new city, taking classes with people I am pretty sure never smelled beer before, let alone partied like I did, and it was getting harder and harder to fake my "good" work. Eventually, I had to face the cold, hard truth . . . I was a terrible graphic designer. I was a terrible illustrative artist. I needed a new career path.

The school had a job fair. I went and I learned about project management. Basically, project managers map out the projects that game designers develop. To understand why these people are so important you have to understand the basics of the gaming industry. Video games have their big companies, the ones you've heard of; Blizzard Entertainment, Ubisoft, and so on. But these are not necessarily the companies that produce the work that makes the games. Ubisoft and the like will subcontract multiple jobs to smaller companies. Those smaller companies then complete the project they are paid for and Ubisoft works as the distributor for the game.

When I found out about the project management gig, I got so giddy you would've thought I had won the lotto. *Wow!* I thought. *No more lying to myself, or having to pay people to do my work for me. This is great!* And it was. But project managers didn't get game art and design degrees. They got business degrees. They got project management degrees. Leadership degrees. It took me about nine months, over $20,000 in tuition, and multiple failed attempts at trying to be something I wasn't to finally understand that while I loved video games I would never design them. Truthfully, I don't remember being that upset. I was kind of relieved. No more faking it.

Until that dream didn't happen either.

So I dropped out. I didn't mind much because now I was available for work. I inherited my father's half of a longtime family-owned pizzeria in Michigan when he died. I was 16 so I wasn't a legal owner, but I would go up there as often as possible so I could learn the ropes of the food industry. At first, I really enjoyed it. Then, I really didn't enjoy it. I wasn't lazy but my heart was not in it. That wasn't the path of my calling.

Then there was property investing. Again, my heart was not in it. After two years I said fuck this, I'm miserable, I'm done. Truth is that my dad wanted me to be a property investor and flip houses. My dad wanted me to take over the pizzeria. My dad drilled all of the secrets of these industries into my head. But it was never what I wanted to do.

Uh, hi, I'll take a large order of depression, cocaine, and, uh, let's see, hm, uh, I mean, I never tried rock . . . Oh, and a side of painkillers. With a large whiskey and beer. Thanks.

Just like that I was back at it. I was fucked up 90 percent of that time between colleges. Whether I was working my pizzeria or investing, I was stoned. Really anything I could get my hands on. I continued a habit of heavily mixing drugs from my teenage years. Coke was always mixed with a painkiller and alcohol. Alcohol was never just alcohol; coke was snowed in. Painkillers alone were probably the most common solo drugs I used. I've looked basically the same since I was 16 and could get into almost any bar, so drinking age or not, I was boozing.

There was a short period where I was not working or in school. During these particular three or four months, I was not really doing anything with my pizzeria.

My first preferred career path was the military. This is totally out of left field because I do not come from a military family. My brother is in the military now but our father desperately tried to get us off that path. He wanted us to forget about it, having a sole life goal in mind—make money. The military didn't offer the millions you could make as an entrepreneur so therefore it was useless, in his eyes.

In this way, he and I are worlds apart. Looking back at my younger years, I think it's fair to suggest some of my materialistic habits came from him. I'm beyond happy I grew out of that.

Of course, the military was not possible due to my amputations. That was one of the hardest blows for me to take, to understand that I would never serve in the military. I even remember being a freshman in high school and looking for loopholes so that I could join as an amputee. I called recruiters regularly and not a single one ever had the heart to tell me the truth. They never said I couldn't join but they didn't lie either. I think someone in the Coast Guard eventually told me, "Look, man, no one is going to be able to take you. It's just the way it is."

I was this pissed-off kid whose dreams of being in the military were destroyed by a car accident, inherited a pizzeria I didn't really want, tried work as a property investor and hated it, and did as much dope as I could get my hands on. I called the DEA. I called Border Patrol. I called ICE. I called the CIA. I never called the FBI but that's a different story. Hit a brick wall everywhere I went.

Alas, not all hope was gone! What's that? Military intelligence? Contracting work for the Department of Defense? Hmm. Tell me more.

I spent an entire night looking into military intelligence work while totally blitzed on blow. Line after line, Google search after Google search, I now had a plan. I would study history and political science and that would be enough for me to get my foot in the door at a defense contracting company. After that, all I needed to do was show good moral fiber, that I had a head on my shoulders, and I'd get my security clearance. Or maybe they would see fit to give me security clearance right away? That'd be amazing! Right out of college and already have a sponsor for my security clearance (that cost upwards of $100,000 at the time)? Fuck ya! I was pretty naïve thinking it would be that simple, but I had a plan and that was all that mattered. Not a realistic plan, but hey, details weren't important at that time.

I was so excited and high, I could hardly tell the difference. While totally tweaking out, I drove to my local university at 9:00 a.m. and said I wanted to register for classes in the upcoming semester. I had to get my transcripts from the Art Institute but that would be easy. I didn't want to retake core classes (math, science, etc.) if I didn't have to, so I got to work. With my luck, only a couple classes transferred. I had to retake most of my core classes.

That decision was made while being totally high. I hardly had a comedown from the drugs because I was so excited to have a plan. It was a plan that I came up with, not one that I felt like I should follow because that was what was expected of me. I really felt like every power in the universe was on my side. I felt closer to God, or whatever powers that be. I was a Satanist at the time, not a Luciferian. Regardless, I was so fucking ready. I was hungry. With Lucifer on my side, nothing would stop me. And nothing has since he has assisted my life, even if I don't always see it.

All the same, there are few moments in my life I can say I was truly far from the Divine. There are few life experiences like detoxing from drugs. It changes your perspective on life because it shows you the viler depths of your own psyche. It shows you a foul you wouldn't find through normal sickness. It's different.

Ask someone who's ever gone through withdrawal from drug addiction if that experience would equate to their understanding of being devoid of the Divine.

Even if they aren't religious, chances are they will agree.

The only divinity found in withdrawing is knowing what it feels like to be void of God (the ALL, the Monad, a Universal Divine, etc.). You will know what it feels like to be starved of light. To explore the new Hell you created. You will understand why Blavatsky spoke so staunchly against drug use. She is right. Indulgence in drugs and alcohol—on a regular and ongoing basis—separates you from the Divine. It blinds you to the gnosis your daemons will attempt to bestow upon you. Not entirely, but it dulls their voice. Why would you ever want to turn down the volume of Divine wisdom?

Drugs and alcohol trap you in the high state—the astral plane—and you won't want to escape. Once you do, that dark place will follow you, as if it is a creature only you can feel, clawing at your very being to be ripped apart.

A phantom psychic vampire of your own creation.

*In 2012 President Obama cut the Department of Defense (DOD) budget in half, and as a result they were laying off people left and right. Those people went to contracting companies that I wanted to work for. So the contracting companies now had this influx of DOD applicants, former military personnel and people with 150+ IQs working for them, or trying to get work from them. A lot of them already had the security clearance. They weren't going to take a fresh college graduate who was a history major with a minor in political science. It was seriously heartbreaking, but I found other paths I could exceed on.

Chapter Six

HUMANISM

"If you knew what I know about the power of giving, you would not let a single meal pass without sharing it in some way."

—Buddha

WHAT DOES IT MEAN TO BE HUMAN?

Should we just look to science for an answer? Is the label of homo sapiens enough?

Does being human mean you possess tribal characteristics? What an American might say makes someone human and what a Russian might say is probably going to be different. So are the shared characteristics of your tribe(s) enough to describe you as a human being?

Is our consciousness what makes us human?

Is thinking, breathing, ingesting enough to make us human?

The Luciferian appreciates the human factor. One should consider that the people you are dealing with are basically animals with natural instincts very much like yours. Understanding human nature is as much a Luciferian practice as any other scientific discovery. Human nature would include psychology and understanding patterns of behavior. None of this is ignored by any esoteric practioner.

I think all of the above are probably true. I don't think there is any one answer to the big human question. Science doesn't explain it fully because at the bare base we are homo sapiens but obviously not all members of the species are the same. When we start to separate our genetic basis the possibilities are endless. It starts off being homo sapiens, then male and female, and before you know it we are separated by our physical characteristics and personality traits.

Maybe being human simply means being an individual. People have a unique genetic make-up and that's what makes them who they are. They way each person thinks, reacts, and relates to distinct situations is what makes them different and because of this no two people are the same. No two people think exactly alike. No two people relate to the same situation in entirely the same way.

Humanism plays a large role in Luciferianism. Humanism promotes the idea of rational thought and scientific discovery. Due to this, religion and humanism have always been at odds with one another. But I don't think they are enemies, even if historically they have been.

Humanism and religion seem to be at odds mostly due to the belief in an afterlife. A Christian believes that they must live a certain way to gain acceptance into heaven. The way they are supposed to live is directly influenced by religious text. Humanism rejects the idea that religion dictates morality. Therefore, humanism rejects the idea of religion because humanists do not think you need religion to live a moral life, whereas theists *typically* believe the opposite.

There is also the issue of human actions. A humanist does not believe in the idea of praising a deity to get something in life. Therefore the humanist will believe that if an individual prays or praises a deity they are wasting their time and energy. Abrahamic religions require praise and prayers. As a Luciferian I do not praise the gods or daemons. I do not pray. I do not engage in ceremonial ritual magick. I see a separation between performing a ritual and prayer but even I'll admit it is a thin line. Regardless, because I do not praise the gods I recognize and just utilize their energy as a beneficial source in my life, I think it is easy to add humanistic ideals into my philosophical practice.

Humanism and religions like Islam or Christianity do not mix. Islam and Christianity essentially say that humans are supposed to live a certain way as foretold by prophets or a messiah. To live outside of these rules is a disgrace to God as far as they are concerned. But Luciferianism has no dogma attached to it.

On top of that, religions generally think in terms of "good" and "evil." You cannot call yourself a Luciferian and think in these terms. Hermeticism shows us there is a duality to all things, and by accepting that, we agree that the two sides of the same coin argument is a constant and repeated theme throughout life.

Actions I would consider "evil" probably aren't evil to those performing those actions. ISIS members think they are doing God's work. So did the Nazis. Mongolians. Hitler. Stalin. Che Guevara. All of these people or groups of people committed their acts thinking they were justified. So while their actions are immoral, or "evil," to me, to the person doing the act they weren't. Those actions were "good" to them.

A guideline is not a rule. While books like Michael Ford's *The Bible of the Adversary* or Anton LaVey's *The Satanic Bible* might seem like any other biblical text, they are really just ideas and guidelines for life and ritualistic practice. *The Bible of the Adversary* has certain "rules" that I do not agree with. That doesn't make me not a Luciferian, it just means I don't consider *The Bible of the Adversary* as absolute law. The same goes for *The Satanic Bible*. Both of them formulate ideas that are intended to help the individual grow but it would be totally absurd to suggest that someone else would dictate the individual Luciferians way of life or say what rules they can and cannot follow (not to say this way of life is a free for all—it most definitely is not).

Humanism relates to Luciferianism directly because we accept and encourage human individuality. In the same way Satanism promotes man as a beast, Luciferianism accepts man and even promotes the idea of exploring mankind's nature and full potential. Understanding man is a never-ending process and will continue to be for the rest of human existence. We will never fully grasp the idea of what it is to be human. The best we can do is speculate and hope we are sort of in the ballpark.

As to my own uniqueness, I can only judge from what others have told me makes me different. I believe people see themselves as more unique than they actually are. I sometimes struggle to understand that situations in my life are not unknown to others—after all, other people have experienced similar situations, trials and accomplishments. In my head, I am unique. I am different. I am the only person who is entirely on my side. In reality my life is not so different from others. We differ in details but more often than not the overall picture is the same.

In any given situation where there is a problem that involves me, I stop to think if I am causing the issue or I am a part of the solution, for both it and me. I ask myself if I am right and justified as opposed to being wrong and arrogant. I consider the concerns of others and look to see if our problems align, because if they do, our solutions will usually align. I do not try to be the nicest person nor am I a pushover for my clients but I am always trying to give them a fair deal. I recognize it is my actions I will be judged on, not the intent. I take full responsibility for my actions and myself at all times, not just when it suits me.

I struggle to fully understand the concept of vulnerability. I am able to bring myself right to the point of addiction and retreat, understanding exactly where the line is. I am able to look at a situation that many would call wrong, immoral, or even illegal, and see it without any of those preconceptions. I can look at something and see it for exactly what it is versus what it is perceived to be. I recognize that because my own morality and that of others will not always align my actions will no doubt confuse and irritate some observers.

From what I have been told my statements above are not common. So that itself is a part of what makes me different. That difference plays a massive role in my personal humanity.

Titles we give ourselves don't make us unique. Calling myself a Luciferian doesn't make me unique. I can declare I am a Luciferian all I want but if I do not adhere to the Luciferian lifestyle and practice, it just words. If my actions don't match the title them the title doesn't matter much to begin with.

Humans cannot only be judged by their individuality. I think our tribe(s) help define us as human beings. Therefore our similarities to our neighbors must be recognized. The similarities we share among our tribe will always dramatically outweigh what makes us unique. We are far more similar to our tribe(s) than we probably care to admit.

Nationally you could see this in America after the 9-11 attacks. The petty differences faded as September 12th, 2001 came and we were unified as a nation. We were fellow Americans and neighbors, nothing else.

Generating another example, I live in a condo. I have seen my next-door neighbor a handful of times. Even though we look different, lead different lives, work different jobs, we are a part of the same tribe and therefore share certain characteristics.

We both pay our very high homeowners' association fees each month. We both go to the same desk to pick up packages and check our mail. We both park on the same level in the parking garage. We both occasionally use the pool, whether to swim, BBQ, use the gym, or the hot tub. We both lose power at the same time. We both lose gas at the same time. We both keep in mind that there is a person living next to us and try not to be excessively loud. We both get annoyed when my dog barks.

I'm also willing to bet that we both are polite to each other because that is what is expected of neighbors. We both smile when we see each other because it is the nice thing to do when you see someone in a hallway. We both have families and friends who visit us. We both bullshit with our coworkers. We both cook for ourselves. We both clean our homes.

I'd guess 99 percent of the similarities I just listed are true for us because we belong to the same tribes. We both live in the same building. We both live in the same city. We probably have a multitude of other similarities on a social basis, which will be undeniably true whether we agree politically, religiously, or in any other way. Because we are both human beings living in a western society.

Being human means you will always make an impact on other people. Every impact you cause will be different as the person you are affecting will see what you do to them differently from someone else. Even if you do the same thing to two different people, at two separate times, both of them will react to your action in a different way. From the cashier at a drug store to the person you hold the door open for. The same action for two different people will be regarded differently, even if it only varies minutely.

I have been close to my sister my entire life. We have always got along. Of course we fought like any siblings have but we are only two and a half years apart. Many of our friends growing up were the same. I always hung with an older crowd, usually around her age. She had been there for me many times.

When our father died I took on any responsibility I could to pick up his slack and help where I could. While she was a college student and living off ramen noodles I would come to her house with groceries for her and her boyfriend. She was always grateful and always answered my 4:00 a.m. drunk calls to let me crash at her place. Least I could do.

I was maybe 19 or 20 when her boyfriend moved out of her place. To keep it she needed more help. We were talking on the phone once and she mentioned it. I offered to cover his share of rent. She refused multiple times but I told her she didn't have an option. I was genuinely happy to help.

Every month from then until her lease ending I sent her money to help with the rent. I never thought twice about it. I never asked her to pay me back. It was my gift to her. We laugh about it now, how she owes me, but we know it's a joke between us and I don't expect her to ever give me back a dime. Nor would I accept it.

Being a humanist doesn't mean you are automatically this fanatically charitable person. It doesn't mean you join the Peace Corps and travel the world to help the indigenous people of wherever. It means that when the opportunity arises for you to empathize with another human, you take advantage of it provided it serves your own interests as well. My personal interest here was helping her in a way my dad might have, thus making me more like him, which at the time was important to me. When you can connect with someone on a deep and personal level, you do. When someone needs a life raft thrown to him or her you toss it out there. Because you too are a human being. You too understand what it means to need help. To need someone to have your back. Someone. Not something. Not some deity or mythical being.

Admittedly, if my sister saw this act as something that God had a hand in, I would be a little annoyed. Undoubtedly this is my ego talking but people seem to be so quick to leave it up to God, or give credit to God, whoever that God is. This didn't have anything to do with any deity. This was one human being acting in empathetic accordance with another human being. God had nothing to do with it.

I have called on the gods many times in my life. When I need to shed light on a situation I am dealing with or need help in more personal ways, I sometimes turn to them. Before that I ensure I explore all human options available to me. Gods cannot do anything except give insight or show us a path we might not immediately recognize. They guide humanity, whether you recognize them or not, but humanity makes the move.

Prometheus gives fire to man. Man uses it. We are where we are today because of that (according to the myth). If Prometheus gave fire to man and we rejected it, well, what good does that do? Prometheus could watch human shivering in the cold, point to his fire gift and tell humanity it will warm them, but humanity has to move towards the fire.

Even my favorite Christians will agree; God has given us everything we need. Use all of it and flourish forward. Stop looking up and start looking side to side.

I assisted my sister because I understood that living off cheap, high-sodium shit was bad for her health. I did what I did because I knew she in school full-time and working part-time. I did it because it was what my father would've done. I did it because I empathized with her situation.

I was 20 when my brother was stationed in Miami. He moved first, then my sister-in-law followed. They were coming from Virginia Beach, Virginia, where a lot of their friends and some of her family lived. He had been in the military for years so he was used to moving around. Still, I wanted to show him around town so he could learn which areas were best.

There's a seven-year difference between my brother and me. At the time we weren't very close. Growing up we were different types of people. To put it as bluntly as I can, imagine your stereotypical jock. That was my brother. Imagine your stereotypical metalhead. That was me. We never really had any issues, it was just that we were into different things, different crowds, we had different ideas of what was fun.

When he moved I was excited to have him so close. I had a chance to finally have a real relationship with my brother. I turned 21 right after he moved so he and I could go to bars together now without the worry of me being carded (wasn't much of a worry but still). I could hang with him and his wife. I could get to know her more as well. This was a golden opportunity for me.

I fucked it up.

In the four years he was stationed in Miami (and lived 20 minutes away) I'd be surprised if I made it over to his house twenty times. It was always a thing of "I'll call him next week." Next week never came and before I knew it he was being stationed out of Florida. I remember trying to fit as many visits as I could into the last couple of months he was there. He was having his first kid and they had a couple of house parties—gender reveal and the baby shower—and I made sure to attend all of them that I possibly could and then some.

I was so ashamed for not taking more initiative to be there while he was here. Yes, this was a busy time for me. Yes, I had a multitude of things going on. But it would've been nothing for me to have him and his wife over for dinner once a month. I beat myself up about missing this opportunity for a long time. Eventually I came to realize that just because I missed that chance doesn't mean I need to miss others. A wasted past doesn't dictate a wasted future. Whether they are holidays, or random calls, I ensure I make time for my brother. He had always been there for me just like my sister. I love him the same. I promised myself I'd be more involved in his life.

Why do I hone in on this particular situation? Because as a humanist I feel like it was a failure. I had the opportunity to be there but chose **insert whatever excuse I gave myself here**. None of those excuses were as important as becoming closer to my brother and his wife. Today our relationship is more solid than it ever has been. I'm happy for it. Turns out being a Puddle Pirate doesn't make you totally lame.

Being a humanist means you also accept other people's failures. I cannot judge someone for failing when I have also been there time and time again. I can and do judge people for not learning from their mistakes but I cannot despise someone for making the mistake in the first place. You're allowed to fuck up at least once.

My failures are mine to keep. I have to embrace the lesson and the failure just as hard as I would embrace the accomplishment. Both have a benefit and a disadvantage and neither can be negated because of what it may teach us. The failures we endure can seem like darkness that is creeping upon us but I have found that light is always at the end of that tunnel. When we fail at a task we often feel defeated and we can loathe the outcome. That's fine. Feel it. Hate that you failed. But never allow the hatred for failure to blind you from learning the lesson you need to face. And most importantly, failure means you tried. You gave it an attempt. The older I get the more I realize many people play it safe. My failures sting a little less recognizing that, even if in the moment I become annoyed.

All the same my accomplishments are mine to keep. Regardless I still recognize the duality that surrounds my accomplishments. It can be difficult for me to explain this because an accomplishment is always accompanied by happiness but I'm still determined to do better at the end of the day.

My previous work as a concert promoter is a good example of this. If I sold out 300 capacity venue for months at a time, at a certain point I have to consider when is it time to find a bigger venue. Why stop growing?

It's not that accomplishments should be look at as "how can I do better?" It's that after something is accomplished I'm always going to consider what the next bigger playing field is. Those thoughts are always on my mind after I make an attempt at something, whether it becomes a success or failure.

I feel humanity can sometimes be satisfied with mediocrity, not feeling the need to want more. Desiring a better outcome, even when your goal is well accomplished, may seem like a negative response to some—but not to me. Be proud, be happy, feel the warmth from earning your reward. But to stop there means that you are not striving for a better result. I think better is always possible. It's what I strive for.

Being a human doesn't mean you have to automatically like someone just because they are from the same species. We judge the way people look, the way they speak, think, act, talk, and engage with one another; we judge based on the tribes people belong to. I see nothing wrong in that. We are raised as individuals and gain a group mentality as we mature. That mind-set keeps us alongside others who think and act like we do. It's a defense mechanism. Even those who seem to float from tribe to tribe and are engaging with specific individuals within those tribes. Each of those individuals is going to carry similar traits.

I can blend with almost any group of people. Growing up I was a hardcore metalhead but in college I joined a fraternity and got along with my fraternity brothers just fine. We had different ideas of what was fun or entertaining but all the same I regularly hung out with them while I was an active member. Recognizing this sort of chameleon effect I possess, the fraternity brothers I got along with best had similar characteristics of the metalhead friends that I am closest to.

As a Luciferian, I follow the idea that the gods promote understanding humanity. Therefore why not try to learn more about our species? Though it is important to take a lesson from Satanism and not forget to embrace the beast within. My favorite quote from Anton LaVey is "There is a beast inside man that should exercised, not exorcised." We should explore this reality. Humanity tries to separate itself far too often from the beast within. But if we stop running from the animal and start to embrace it, we can understand our primal selves even further.

Trust me, that is always a positive.

CHAPTER SEVEN

DETERMINATION

"In the absence of willpower the most complete collection of virtues and talents is wholly worthless."

—ALEISTER CROWLEY

FEELING DETERMINED IS POSSIBLY the greatest feeling in the world. The amount of focus, will, and strength it requires is the best test you can put yourself through. It rarely comes without struggle but ideally you will face a new mental war to challenge yourself.

I've learned the hard way that happiness is not always the goal but rather satisfaction. Attempting to remain happy, or satisfied, requires us to be determined to live a better life than we have thus far. Determination is the reason we accomplish goals, big and small—but also why being content with our current position rarely lasts long.

Determination is the answer to everything in this book, should there be a question. Why did I go back to college? Because I was determined to live a life I planned for myself. Why is it important for me to ensure that I take at least some responsibility for how others view me as an amputee? Because I am determined to not let my disability define my identity. Why did I get my truck slammed into when I was 16? Because I was determined to get high.

I often find myself amazed at some people's lack of determination. I do not understand how they choose to sideline the most important details of their life so they can focus on what's unimportant. We all do this at times, but the person who consistently refuses to do the necessary things for living a better life makes no sense to me.

People have been telling me since I was 11 that I inspire them. I guess I sort of understand but at the same time I don't. No one ever really told me what it was that I inspired them to do so that's part of my confusion. Granted, I take a shit and some people will still be inspired.

Wow, see that guy, he has no legs and he can wipe his ass! I swear some people think this.

I don't get it. But maybe I don't need to. Maybe their threshold for what inspires them is lower than mine and therefore virtually anything I do will inspire them.

Some amputees do amazing things to defeat their disability. I applaud these people but I don't know if I would say they inspire me, least not in the way I inspire able-bodied people. I'm inspired by anyone with superior athletic skills. Crippled or not, if you can run and finish a marathon or triathlon then I am going to be inspired by your accomplishment. The unilateral, above-knee amputee who completes a full marathon is always going to inspire some people and it is simple to understand why. But I feel the same way about them as I do about an able-bodied person who does the same.

If I had to guess, I inspire others so much because I am able to live independently as an amputee and they cannot imagine being able to do that or don't think they would even try. It took time to get accustomed to everything, sure, but it's not impossible to live well as an amputee or wheelchair-bound for that matter. And for those who can't imagine even trying, of course they would try—and see success with some things and failure with others. I don't know any person who lost a limb and became suicidal because of it though that seems to be what most people believe would happen to them.

I was lucky. I lost my legs at 11 and now, at 33, I don't remember too much of what it was like to live with them. I used to ride my bike a lot but apart from that I don't remember having legs a whole lot (or rather, I don't remember *appreciating* them). The person who lost a limb at 26 is really the one with the uphill battle. They are the ones who should inspire you. They will endure phantom pain (feeling like your limb is still there—sensation can be like an itch or burn) for much longer than I ever had to. Granted I still feel it every now and again but it comes fast and goes fast. They will have to deal with it more intensely for the rest of their lives. They have more memories of walking. I don't have those issues because it happened when I was young.

Inspiration drives determination but it is not the only thing that can do so. Sometimes pain is the driver.

My Uncle Pat died from diabetes. Over the course of 12 years, piece by piece, he had more and more parts of him amputated. It started with a toe, then half a foot, then the entire foot, then the leg below the knee, and so on. When he died he was a bilateral-amputee. It tore up my family to see him in this state. To watch someone close to us deteriorate so traumatically.

His diabetes was brought on by a life of eating poorly. When he died I had my own wake-up call. I don't have much else to take in the limbs department. I knew I needed to change my lifestyle and my choices or I would suffer a similar fate. It took years to get it right, but this scared me for my own weight issues. I didn't take my weight problems seriously until he died.

I was incredibly hurt by my uncle's death. He had become close to me after my dad passed away and he and I shared a similar circumstance. Amputees, like people who are wheelchair-bound, share a sort of common understanding about the world and to have that bond with my uncle was important to me.

His death was a mournful experience to deal with but it skyrocketed my determination. It is terrible that had to happen for me to realize what I had to do but I am further along in my fitness goals today because of it.

Overall determination in the long-term is not a conscious thought. Our actions work toward our desired goal and it is action itself that is the determination. These actions, influenced by my philosophical ideals, drive my life forward. Everything we do is driven by our determination, whether we realize it or not.

You go to school and major in biology because you want to be a veterinarian. You go to work because you want to get paid. You take your partner on a date because you want to spend quality time with them. Your actions are working toward your long-term goal and you are determined to make it happen.

But what happens when we lose that determination?

I was in the second semester of my junior year in my undergrad course and I was losing the motivation to finish school. I didn't see the point any more. President Obama's budget cuts meant I would never work in military intelligence. Too much competition and I had no experience. I considered lobbying for a while—but who am I kidding?—I don't like people enough to put the energy into constantly hammering at them to join my cause. I thought about being a high school history teacher until I learned from my old history teacher that they can force you to teach incorrect or incomplete lessons. I considered being a rock music historian but even though I would have really enjoyed such a career there isn't a demand for it. I can think of maybe two rock historians and even they don't have many books out on the subject.

It started to show in my schoolwork. At this point I was constantly thinking about dropping out. Why bother any more? What's the point? The only thing that was really keeping me in college was I knew that a bachelor's degree would serve me well. I finally figured I would regret not finishing school.

I did finish that year and got okay grades. I had always been a B or C student with a couple As sprinkled in there. It all depended on how interested I was in the course. But over the summer break I started to lean more and more toward the drop-out side.

Over that summer I went to a concert—which will feature in a later chapter. That event started a ripple effect that changed my life and career goals. I still considered history-related options in my senior year but the idea of working in the music industry was suddenly so much sweeter to me. This story of determination is to be continued . . .

I worked as a piercing artist for two years. I started my apprenticeship in 2012 under a well-known and well-respected body modification artist named Pinhead. I did my apprenticeship at a beach shop. Beach shops get a bunch of walk-in traffic and I had numerous friends come and see me to get pierced. With this much constant practice on willing pincushions it wasn't long before I was a licensed piercing artist.

My initial goal of working in the shop wasn't to be a piercing artist. This was during the boom of tattoo studios. There seemed to be a new reality show every day on tattooing, new shops were popping up left and right, tattoos as a whole were becoming more and more accepted. I wanted to cash in on this and open a studio. I knew I didn't want to work as a full-time investor anymore but I also wanted to see my assets grow. Problem was I knew absolutely nothing about the industry. You can't rely on a scripted "reality" television show to explain how a shop's day-to-day operations work.

I got my first piercing, a labret (middle of bottom lip), after my dad died. I never wanted my ears pierced because I thought it was one of the gayest things a guy could do. Then I turned 21 and said "hey, why not?" and went to get them done. I found Pinhead through an online search. I go into the shop, get them done, and he and I really hit it off. I started to pick his brain apart a bit and he gave me some useful information on the industry and how to get in without artistic talent, which I didn't have.

Piercing is more of a medical procedure than it is an art. You can definitely do some artistic designs with a piercing—or rather multiple piercings—but most of it is hygienic practice, how to set up a clean work station, make sure you aren't torturing your client, how to get the needle straight, stuff like that.

Another visit for another piercing and I asked Pinhead how I could apprentice under him. A couple months later I did, with the end goal of opening my own studio and cashing in on the booming industry trend.

I was incredibly determined to open a shop. As I apprenticed I soaked up everything I could about the industry. One small problem though; I had never been an employee before. I worked for my uncle at the pizzeria but I was its coowner. I answered to him and the manager but it's not like it was a secret that I had pull in that establishment.

As a result, I didn't understand my place in the work hierarchy. I paid for my apprenticeship and I paid a lot. I thought that meant I was on equal playing field as those who were there before me.

I wasn't.

I was still a lowly apprentice. When issues started to arise with scheduling, the other piercing artists, and the owner, I didn't back down or stay quiet. I fully take responsibility and realize that I was too cocky for my own good. I understand that the way I spoke to the shop owner and other artists who'd been there long before me was wrong. Not even because I was an apprentice but just for keeping the workplace civil.

Piercing artists, tattoo artists, they aren't technically employees. I thought that because I was technically an independent contractor I didn't need to take shit from these people and could talk to them like we were in a kitchen instead of a tattoo studio (if you've worked in a kitchen, you'll understand). I also, very arrogantly, thought that because the industry was one that could be considered "alternative" it meant that professionalism between coworkers could be bent (I think it's common sense that professionalism to clients is necessary in any type of work). That was wrong of me. This was the education I didn't get.

I paid for a year apprenticeship under Pinhead, one of the most well-known piercing artists in Florida at the time. I got two months with him before he quit a shop where he'd worked for over 10 years because the owner never paid him for my apprenticeship, meaning he was teaching me for free. His right-hand man followed him out, who also learned under him and would've been a great replacement mentor. This pissed me off because I paid so much for the apprenticeship under him and had it finished by a piercing artist who was just waiting for a tattoo artist position to open up so he could return to tattooing. A lot of what he told me flatly contradicted Pinhead's instruction and honestly, fuck him. Pinhead could run rings around this asshole and now I am supposed to take his word for everything? No, I'm good.

Anyway, I was getting in trouble because I did things Pinhead's way and not my new mentor's, who for whatever reason never seemed to like Pinhead. Pinhead was one of the kindest people I've ever met (he died years ago). I just figured it was an ego thing on his end.

The shop where Pinhead went was welcoming and friendly to me. I never technically worked there but I did take an appointment there from time to time. Any instruction I asked Pinhead or the other piercing artists there about was always answered. I always appreciated that.

I eventually quit the beach shop and didn't work as a piercing artist again for a couple of months. When I got a new job at a far superior studio, I had lost my interest in opening a shop. At this point I just wanted to gain back my initial investment for my apprenticeship. And I won't lie; it's a fun industry to be a part of. On top of this I would go to work and do my schoolwork or handle other projects while there. Tattoo artists in their off time can draw to get better at their craft. Piercing artists can only do so much without something to practice on, so in my downtime I was doing the same thing there I would've done at home. It was a win-win for me to continue to work in that field.

I was maybe six months or so from the start of my apprenticeship and this place didn't have the walk-in traffic of the beach shop.

At this new shop I had none of the same problems, fortunately. I'd learned my lesson and was careful to take a new approach to working this closely with people. I tried to be as professional as possible with everyone. Though I still made stupid mistakes. I was still learning the tools of the trade—and how to work with an employee mind-set.

I got another job at a different studio and worked both. The new place was less prestigious but I made more money there. There was a bit more walk-in traffic and I enjoyed the people I worked with more. One of the owners was a close friend so working there was easy. We never found ourselves at odds over work-related issues.

My boss at the prestigious shop and I were always butting heads. He had this sort of nerd chip on his shoulder and I thought he was as much of an idiot as he obviously thought I was. He liked to insult me somewhat regularly in front of or to clients, which I obviously didn't appreciate. He was an extremely well accomplished tattoo artist and I think it just went to his head after a while. Lacking his own insight, he never realized how disliked he was by other people who worked at different shops. I would regularly hear the echo of my own feelings toward him said by others who knew of him. To be fair, and possibly rightfully so, their opinions of him, like mine, don't mean anything. But if you're going to conduct yourself as a professional in your industry perhaps it would be beneficial to understand how you come off to others.

The walk-in heavy shop shut down after six months of my employment. I went back to full-time at the prestigious shop. Tensions were high between my employer and me. We simply just didn't like or respect one another. Even to this day if someone were to ask me to envision smugness, he immediately comes to mind. The silent partner in that shop and I downright hated each other's guts. I have never met someone on such a power trip nor have I ever seen someone act so aggressively in the workplace. Again, not saying I was the model employee because I wasn't, but this guy was an insufferable ass. Under the circumstances it surprised me that nobody told me I was fired on a whim.

I graduated from my undergraduate program and was headed to grad school shortly after. I told the shop manager I was putting in my two-week notice but I never directly told the shop owner. When I finally informed him he said the manager had told him. He asked if I was going to continue piercing once I was in grad school; I said I wasn't. He surprised me by adding he thought it was a good idea because I wasn't determined anymore. I admitted I had lost my initial enthusiasm and drive somewhere along the line, which was true, but I bit my tongue about what I really thought about him and his studio. And honestly, I regret it. I was leaving his studio and the industry as a whole. I didn't need a nice send-off with the handshake between us. Asking him to repeat some of the insanely disrespectful things he said to me again, now that he couldn't hold my job over my head, would be a far nicer memory. The only reason he got away with treating people like he did was because of his position in the industry. I didn't give a shit about his position anymore, but I did care about my professional profile. While I can applaud my younger self for this in some way, sometimes the soul will thrive more from telling someone to rightfully go fuck themselves. Lesson learned.

I understand the obvious answer here is I should've left long before it got this far but understand, this was a seemingly good opportunity. I was working alongside giants in the tattoo industry. While I can look back and see how it meant nothing for me—as a piercing artist—at the time it seemed like a much bigger deal. The point of getting a job is to keep it. This industry in particular has an employee's jumping-from-shop-to-shop issue. So I stayed. But when workplace dissatisfaction turned to blatant disrespect, I had no business sticking around. My performance reflected that reality.

I hadn't really thought about it like that until he said it. I wasn't determined to open a shop any more, that goal was long gone. I only kept doing it to retain the money I had initially put up. I was still determined to be a better piercing artist but as soon as the opportunity came to start my career in music I didn't even think for one nanosecond that I was going to miss the piercing business. I could've got a job in the city where I was doing my graduate program. I got a job offer while I was there visiting some friends at their studio. But I had zero interest.

My osseointegration experience is another example of my determination. Though, unlike piercing or college, this was something I knew I wouldn't quit once I had started.

Spending all these years in my wheelchair got me awfully comfortable to it. I've figured out all the ways to get around efficiently. I'm fast in my chair. I can wheel around all day and the only issues I'll have are light back pain, which isn't uncommon for any daily user. Wheeling around definitely doesn't help my shoulder pain either but I've lived with it long enough to where I can brush it off most of the time.

Prior to getting osseointegration I was determined to walk. It became this constant thought in the back of my mind. I knew what I had to do to get it done and started to build the plan to move forward. From the time I heard about the procedure until the time I got it done was about three years. For the first year I didn't know if I would be a candidate. Then I met the doctor and spoke to him about my concerns. Immediately he cleared me.

Okay, now this is real. Now this is a possibility, I thought.

Osseointegration didn't have FDA approval at the time so that meant I would have to raise the funds on my own. I didn't have health insurance so the prosthetics would have to be paid out-of-pocket. Plus, I had to get there. It was extremely expensive.

(2024 side note—osseointegration now has FDA approval in America. Walk on, fellow amputees!)

It took over two years to come up with the money and when I moved out of my house in Fort Lauderdale, part of that decision was so I could get the last bit of money I needed. I was tired of waiting and penny pinching. I needed to take the leap.

One night in early January 2017, I got the call from the Australian group that does this procedure. My date was set. February 13, 2017.

I really don't know if words can express how I felt. Three years of living that fantasy and here it was. In six short weeks I would be getting osseointegration and have an opportunity to walk. Before osseointegration I was fully convinced it would never happen.

It was happening.

The day came and I went to airport. I was on my way to Australia. Fuck yeah!

I arrived and immediately saw doctors and met my physical therapists. They wasted no time, which I was cool with. The first two days were really nothing but appointments. Over the weekend before I got the surgery I found a metal show and went. I headbanged. I talked to some of the local bands on the show. I met a new friend and met up with him a couple weeks later in downtown Sydney.

February 13th came and just like I'm sure most people feel before they get this surgery, it took for-fucking-ever. Hurry up and wait. After what seemed like hours (it wasn't) the doctors came in and I was being wheeled into the surgery room.

The vast majority of the people who get this surgery get an epidural. Can't have your limb twitching as it is being drilled into. The scar tissue on my back made this a difficult task and after four attempts the doctors asked me if I was okay with not doing it. I asked how necessary it was. They said it's just a safety precaution.

Oh, well, as long as it isn't anything important.

I woke up to a nurse tending to me while one of the doctors from the surgery was still with me. I was on morphine, ketamine, antibiotics, and probably sixteen other kinds of drugs so I was pretty loopy. I saw the doctor who preforms the surgery in my room and I asked him if I broke my leg during the procedure, which he said happens to 25 percent of patients. He said no, everything went well, and left.

Over the following three days I went from being extremely excited about all of this to being quite the miserable dick. Those poor nurses had to deal with me constantly begging them to let me get out of the hospital room for a bit. I didn't mean to be an asshole but I've had enough nights spent in a hospital for three lifetimes. It's boring. It's annoying. You're constantly being fucked with. I wanted out. Luckily I had a morphine drip button and whenever it got too boring or painful, I just hit the button. Night night.

Fortunately the pain wasn't too bad, just muscle soreness you could expect after a good workout. After three days I was finally released and went back to my suite.

It is ten days from the surgery until you can start weight-bearing. In the week before I started weight-bearing the pain came. And it sucked. Of course this was all expected but it doesn't mean the reality of dealing with it isn't a pain in the ass.

None of this is to say I didn't feel exceptionally accomplished. I did it. I got the osseointegration procedure. I would walk. My wheelchair, which really became a part of me, was going to be a thing of the past. It would take time but I was trading in the TiLite—the brand of wheelchair I use—for the C-Leg.

Ideally an osseointegration patient will stay in Australia for five weeks. I was there for three weeks. I have a company to run and my clients needed me. From the point of weight-bearing to me leaving was a major emotional rollercoaster.

First, the pain only got worse. I truly have nothing but good things to say about the doctor and all of the people I met and worked with, with the exception of the pain management team. Fuck them. I was given 10mg time-release opiates and nerve blockers for having metal rods shoved into my femurs. It hurt. It was legitimate. But I guess they, like the doctors who I came home to, thought I was just drug seeking.

Well, yeah, I was. There's a reason they call opiates "painkillers."

I didn't care what drugs they were giving me so long as they worked. The nerve blockers weren't doing anything. At one point I was taking double the recommended dose, as suggested by the pain management doctor. No relief and I still couldn't get them to prescribe me opiates.

At least two of the nights I was there the agony was so bad I crushed up the time-release pills and snorted them, recognizing it will have an immediate effect versus waiting for them to kick in. It helped just enough so I was only in bed crying in pain for an hour before I could sleep versus not sleeping at all, which was much worse.

Truthfully it all happened so quick and so slow at the same time. When I was in my suite time couldn't fly fast enough. When I was out of my suite time flew like a jet. Two hours of physical therapy went by extremely fast. I was always upset when it was over. Working with the therapist took my mind off of the pain and reminded me why I was there.

I was still happy I did it. I was still excited. But I was also drained. I was tired all the time. I always had some kind of pain issue.

I remember the first time I stood up on the prosthetics. It was unreal. Not only did standing *completely* take away the pain, it was the entire reason I was there! I don't think I ever walked more than 20–30 feet at a time but I didn't care . . . I was walking! And it was painless. There was no socket pinching my ballsack. There were no liners to deal with. There was only standing on my bone.

It was those moments that made that trip seem worth it. If you were to combine the time I was actually standing or walking throughout the entire trip, I'd be surprised if it was more than three hours. Though those three hours were extremely emotional for me. I'm pretty macho so I wasn't tearing up in front of my therapists, but on numerous occasions I would get back to my suite and cry tears of joy.

Two days before I was set to leave I was at physical therapy and getting set up to stand up and walk. I had already been at therapy for a half hour or so. I planted my arms on the parallel bars and went to stand. I felt a sharp pop in my left leg. I thought I broke it. I sat down and put pressure on my leg. What the fuck just happened?

I couldn't stand again and my pain had skyrocketed. The following day I went and got X-rays. Whether it was from the actual osseointegration surgery or from something I did wrong when standing, I had a hairline fracture in my left leg. No walking for six weeks.

Even writing this I feel my blood starting to boil. I was fucking *pissed*. There was no one to blame, sometimes these things just happen, but *what the fuck*. First the pain and now a hairline fracture that was going to set me back for six weeks?

The night I found out I went to the Sydney Opera House. I didn't do much sightseeing while there and needed to get out of my hotel suite. It was gorgeous and I realized something . . . hairline fracture or not, I had it done. All of the work I put into this and I got it done. I was in the back of the opera house and while looking at it, I felt pretty accomplished. I just took a life-changing risk to give me an opportunity I gave up on for over a decade. I made it. I did everything I had to, dealt with all the headaches, the doctors' appointments, the physical therapy, the pain, the disappointment of the news about my fracture, but I had it done.

Looking at the opera house I simply didn't care about the fracture.

I originally planned on taking my brother with me but from the point of setting the appointment to me leaving was only six weeks. I knew he wouldn't be able to join me. So instead of doing the responsible and smart thing like telling people, I told no one. The only people who knew I was leaving the country and why were my clients, a couple friends, and the doctor. I remember thinking I didn't want anyone there and up my ass. I wanted to do this on my own.

And I did. And even though bringing someone would've been really helpful at times, I still got a sense of accomplishment from not bringing anyone. I don't know exactly why but it felt good to know I took that risk by myself. That's one of the exciting things about determination. It usual involves a risk.

Leaving the opera house I had a changed perspective about it all. Yes, I was still in pain. Yes, I had to deal with this setback. But it was a setback, not something permanent. I could walk now. One day I would be a full-time walker. With that the health risks of being confined to a wheelchair would fade.

I set out to accomplish something for the material but reached a higher level of self through it. Another example of heightened spirituality through physical means. Another example that the Divine can be found in all things, including your determined actions.

Determination is a beautiful emotion. The desire for something better keeps us going and without it I'm not sure what life would look like. I am always going to be determined for more, determined for something better, determined to reach new heights in my personal and work life. We have to remember that determination is the base and willpower and discipline is the force.

My Luciferian belief structure is what underpins all my actions. And with the gods on my side . . . how much more can I get done?

*Please note; if you are an amputee and considering getting the osseointegration surgery, do it. I have spoken to and met many individuals who got the procedure. My situation was not common.

The pain issues I had to deal with were mostly from nerve damage, which I have since had surgery to fix. Nerve damage is a risk that can come from any kind of surgical procedure. Some get it, some don't. But as I slowly gain more and more confidence walking, and as I slowly gain the strength to walk further and further, there is not a single agonizing night I had to deal with in Australia or in the U.S. that isn't worth it.

CHAPTER EIGHT

FEAR

*"If you are possessed of Fear,
do not waste time trying to "kill out" Fear,
but instead cultivate the quality of Courage,
and the Fear will disappear."*

—Three Initiates
The Kybalion

FEAR IS MY FAVORITE EMOTION.

Why?

Because fear demands immediate action.

Rage, confusion, and determination all require action but fear is the quickest way to get a reaction. Humans usually hate fear. Understandably, of course, because fear is the unknown. It is one of the only emotions that makes us worry about whatever will come next.

When we are children we are too afraid to confront our fears. The bump in the night, the monster in the closet, the creaking in the hallway . . . we don't confront such terrors. We feel paralyzed by them. The most we can make ourselves do is tell our parents. When we become adults that same strategy doesn't work.

Granted, as adults we aren't scared of the monster in the closet. We are scared of the monster in people. The woman walking alone at night is scared of being attacked. The man who thinks his family is in danger is scared for their lives. As adults we still believe in monsters, we just also believe that those monsters look a lot like us. We aren't worried about the bogeyman. We fear John Doe down the street and the way he looks at our daughter. We aren't scared of the dark. We are scared of what people do in the dark.

Courage is the obvious answer to fear, but I know for myself it is a reaction that has rarely exposed itself in a triumphant fashion.

Back in high school I wrestled for three years. I didn't finish my third year. I was in the 215 (190-215 lb) weight class, which was *way* above what I should've been (I was a massively overweight kid). My wrestling career went 0 wins 17 losses. But I did it, enjoyed it, and found it useful. I was inspired after reading Kyle Maynard's *No Excuses* where he discusses his wrestling experiences as a quad amputee (no arms, no legs). He was a state champion. He was, in many ways, the start of my venture into self-defense.

Maybe you've heard the term "fight or flight." If you haven't, basically it means that when confronted with a threat people either fight the threat or run from it. There's also freezing, not doing anything at all, but that's just the precursor to the flight or fight response. Keep this in mind. . . .

Wrestling gave me a beautiful introduction to the tools I need to not become a victim. To fight threats that might confront me. At some point in my wrestling career I realized if I am confronted with a threat running is not an option for me. Your standard wheelchair can't outrun a person. Being in high school I was not able to carry a firearm or blade like I do today, but I at least knew what to do if I got in a fight and was taken to the ground, which is exactly what has happened in every fight I've ever gotten into.

Because flight is not an option I had to consider what else I could do. Do nothing? Well, doing nothing is volunteering to be a victim (remember, there are no victims—only volunteers). Or fight? Fighting is the only viable option I have if faced with very real and present danger.

This led to years of sweat, determination, learning, and thousands of dollars invested in my training. I decided to energize the fear of threats with learning to fight. If I am threatened, or someone I love is menaced, it is my responsibility to handle the threat appropriately. No one's coming to save me. I had to learn to save myself.

The gods guided me the entire way. They shed light on the issue. They have shed light on the solution. I am prepared to face the fear of my life of being badly injured now because I've acquired my skills through defensive training. It doesn't mean I won't experience fear. It just means I am not paralyzed by the thought of it. I had the sense and courage to recognize the solution.

Let's call out the obvious: I'm kind of at a disadvantage. Being in a wheelchair opens you up to a variety of issues in a fight. Though I think most people would be surprised to hear this, there are some benefits, but they are obviously going to be very few.

If you take any random ten guys off the street, seven of them can kick my ass on any given day. I'm not delusional. But that's seven, not ten, and I'm proud of the three I could stand a chance against. I'm able to have that chance due to extensive training.

Kyle Maynard was my first inspiration to explore self-defensive measures but he certainly wasn't the last. Meet Amanda.

Amanda was a friend of mine when I was a teen. Pretty girl, couple of years older than me. We used to hang out and play video games with our group of friends. She was married to a guy named Rick but I almost never saw him around. Apparently he worked a lot—and truthfully, their marriage never looked all that good to begin with. They often fought and who wants to listen to that?

I was 16 when I went to Amanda's house to pick her up for a party. Ever enter a room and literally feel the tension before you even talk to someone? Rick was home, sitting on the couch. I looked at him as I followed Amanda inside and said hello. The look he shot back at me made it extremely clear he did not want me there.

Amanda was attempting to act like everything was cool but she was in a hurry to leave. She grabbed her purse, but then forgot her wallet. She grabbed her wallet, but then forgot her phone. She grabbed her phone, and Rick spoke up.

"Where the fuck you think you're going?"

I noticed Amanda's neck was red. She was always well groomed but her shirt was stretched out. I realized Rick didn't want me there because before I arrived he was beating her ass.

This was a new situation. I didn't know what to do. I positioned myself so I could keep an eye on both of them. I didn't say anything. Something told me speaking up would've infuriated Rick and that was the last thing I wanted to do. Rick was a very large, seriously muscular man who had at least one assault charge I knew of.

"I told you I'm going to Gary's house for a party," Amanda said quietly while looking at the ground.

My blood started to boil. My hands began to shake. This fucking pig, low-life, sack of shit. I gritted my teeth.

"Oh and you already got a new dick, fresh and ready to pick you up!" Rick turned to me. "You fucking my wife, cripple boy?"

I looked at him and said, "no."

"Ya you wish, faggot." He stood up and went up to her. He tried to grab her purse but she clenched it while still staring at the floor. "Give me your fucking purse! You're not going anywhere!"

She tried to hold onto it but he overpowered her. He threw the purse across the room and all its contents flew out.

I was frozen. I didn't know what to do. Get involved? Call for help? What do you do when you see this train starting to wreck but don't feel like you can do anything to stop it? Just let it happen? Just let your friend get her ass beaten by this sack of shit? I had a million thoughts run through my head but stayed totally still as I watched Rick.

This is the freeze response.

I was absolutely terrified. Not for myself. I was scared for her.

Rick pushed her hard into the wall that separated the dining room they were standing in and the kitchen. Amanda weighed maybe 115 soaking wet. Rick was maybe 220, tall, muscular. This wasn't a fair fight. I had to step in.

Before I crossed the room he hacked phlegm in her face and called her a vicious cunt. I tried to get between them but Rick stiff-armed me. He had her pinned against the wall by her neck with his other arm. I tried to get his arm off my chest but it wasn't working. No matter which way I tried to push his arm off it remained in the center of my chest. And poor Amanda, she was sobbing while he continued to tell her she was everything she wasn't.

As far as I knew, she never cheated on this guy. And even if she did I don't blame her. Fuck this asshole.

Rick grabbed her by the neck and slammed her head back against the wall before letting go. I told him to leave repeatedly. He did. Though I don't think my recommendation made much of an impression. This fight got loud quick. Someone somewhere was bound to hear it. I think Rick recognized this and that was why he left.

Amanda fell to the floor. I tried to lift her up but she was coughing and it was obviously not a good time to touch her. I looked at the door. I remember thinking, *what the fuck just happened?*

She lived in a condo and one of the neighbors called the cops. While she sat there on the ground I leaned on the dining room table and put my head in my hands. Shortly after Rick left the cops showed up.

I didn't realize it at the time but they must have been there before because they looked right at me, then right at her, and ran up to her. I backed away from the table as they approached her. They knew I wasn't the reason she was beaten and on the floor. She immediately looked at me and shook her head. I took that to mean she wanted me to stay silent.

Cops knew what happened. It was obvious. I didn't open my mouth though. Amanda was betrayed by a man she once loved. I didn't think it was a smart idea for me to betray her too. Whether that was right or wrong is up to you to judge. After the cops left I told her she needs to leave him and get a restraining order. She said she knew, she would, it was time, etc.

I went home and felt like the smallest man in the world. Not only had I just watched my friend get abused, something I hadn't seen (at least not in a marital sense) before but I was totally unable to help. I was useless. There was another consideration: If Rick really thought she was cheating and then I showed up when tensions were high, I might've made the situation worse.

I talked to her later in the night letting her know how sorry I was about it all. I offered my ears in case she needed to vent and I offered my shoulder in case she needed to cry. As selfish it might seem, I needed a shoulder to cry on too. Our relationship was always platonic but Amanda was a good friend and good person. She didn't deserve that.

I replayed the situation in my head a million times. I kept trying to think of the perfect way to handle it. "What if I did this?" "What if I did that?" "What if I did this, then that happened, then I responded with this?" It went on and on and on for a couple days.

I'll never forget that fear. If Rick had punched her just once he could easily have broken something. If he punched me the same would've happened. Yes, I tried to get between them but I didn't. Even the best intentions don't matter if the action falls short. I failed to protect and help someone I cared about because I was too weak, too timid, to slow to react. Obviously 16 year-old, wheelchair-bound me isn't going to do anything against a grown man, but at the time this was how I felt about it.

After that I started carrying a blade everywhere I went, realizing how defenseless I was. I had to ask myself when it is appropriate for me to get involved and when it isn't. Amanda and Rick got back together and I heard it took two more of those traumatic scenes for her to leave him. This isn't to say she is to blame, because she isn't, but she is responsible for her own safety. And when I was put in a situation where I had to consider the safety of a friend, a friend I feared for, I couldn't do anything to help.

That fear made me realize two things; first, I am no one's savior and it is not my job to be a white knight and save anyone from an abusive partner. However, if I have it in my ability to help someone I care about in that situation, I can't just sit back and let that happen. You can't say you care about someone but sit back while you watch them get attacked. Second, I was a weak, underprepared child who needed to learn how to handle such high-risk scenarios. What if Rick turned his anger on me? What would I have done other than sit there and take it? I would've been fucked.

I had two years of wrestling under my belt but that didn't mean shit when I was towered over by that asshole. I tried various things I learned in wrestling to get his arm off my chest to try to get between him and Amanda. None of it worked. So my wrestling skills, in this situation, were entirely useless. They didn't do anything to help Amanda. They didn't do jack shit to defuse or stop the abuse. Which made me realize wrestling was not enough. It was never going to be enough.

We have two very different kinds of fear. One is for yourself. One is for someone else. I'm developed enough to defend myself against outside threats. Not saying I'm some kind of master in self-defense or invincible, but I feel I know enough to defend myself appropriately against most common physical threats. Of course I will always have more to learn and any skills I've developed can be further developed. I'm by no means saying I'm good at self-defense, there's plenty more to learn and train, but I've done a lot so far. My physical strength is an asset that greatly helps complement my defensive abilities.

At the time I originally wrote this, I had seen a therapist regularly for over a year.

At some point I confided I was bored with my life. Work was fun but that wasn't enough of a challenge or variety to make it exciting.

The vast majority of my work was spent sitting behind a computer and organizing concerts. That year I only booked 40 shows. So there are only, maybe, two months out of the year I had to leave my home for work-related reasons. I definitely got cabin fever at times. I used to be a highly reckless individual. I loved it. A lot of that recklessness led me into illegal behavior. I'm too old for that nonsense.

She suggested that due to my previous recklessness I should seek out high-adrenaline activities. Not illegal, and the worst thing that can happen to you is death, or being left paralyzed, or in a coma. Forgetting that in hindsight my therapist might have been trying to kill me, it was a great idea that I agreed to. Problem was that I was still dealing with a lot of pain from osseointegration at the time. I told her I would be more interested in seeking those activities out when I was healed. As I began to heal more, I started to realize something . . .

It seemed to be less of an adrenaline-seeking desire as it was a fear-seeking desire. Maybe they're the same thing. Heights have never really scared me. I went to the Empire State Building once, looked over the rail, and it had no effect on me. I rock climbed once and that too had no effect on me. Both of those activities happened when I was much younger. So for me to experience fear I have to be more than just up high. It has to have the added element of potential danger. Like jumping out of a plane. There's no guarantee that the parachute will work. Or that I won't come undone from the instructor and splatter like a water balloon on someone's nice, clean lawn. What is guaranteed though is that I will be afraid—maybe horribly afraid—of doing it.

I'm not sure why I am so interested in experiencing fear. Maybe because experiencing these near-phobias would mean that by feeling them so intensely they'd be purged out of me. If I ever do skydive and live, well, that isn't much of a fear anymore. I did it. It's no longer unknown.

And let's be honest, just because it worked out once doesn't mean it will always work out the same way. When I originally wrote this, my femur break was only a couple months behind me. I was terrified of falling again. Still am. But I do it, very cautiously, and every time I walk I get a little better at it. Doesn't mean I don't experience fear. But to think that just because something horrible has happened once means it won't happen again is unrealistic. I am 100 percent capable of breaking my leg again. Falling while walking on prosthetics is not impossible today just as it wasn't impossible when it happened. I just have to be cautious and properly train so it doesn't happen again.

I suspended by hooks a couple times. What I did is called a "suicide suspension." The practice is piercing your back, attaching it to a rig, and pulling you up by the piercings. A pretty terrifying thought but after Pinhead died, who was a big fan of this practice, I decided to try it in his memory.

The first two times I did it I got four piercings in my back with 8 gauge needles. If you don't know, that's pretty thick. I came to find out I have pretty tough skin because both times my skin "bit the needle," meaning that as the needle was passing through my skin the tip of the needle bent, basically meaning that razor-sharp edge disappeared mid-piercing. Not as much fun as it may sound.

When that rig is being set up, and you feel your skin pulling, your heart rate will spike. Every nerve is on edge and you are hyper alert to everything around you. It's terrifying. It's not just what if my skin rips, it's what if the rig malfunctions? But I didn't just get pierced four times for nothing. I was going up. Slowly the person who performs this act starts to pull on the rope that the rig is attached to.

Most people, myself included, find that the hardest part is getting off the ground. At that point you are officially being hung by your skin. Most people also have feet so they can ease into it on their toes. I don't have that option so as I was being lifted I had to face it a bit more head on. I looked at the person who performs this act and told him to pull.

I was lifted out of my chair and swung forward. I was being suspended by four piercings in my back. It was a strange feeling, like you're going to fall but it never happens. Believe it or not it doesn't hurt anywhere near as bad as you might expect it to. I swung back and forth for maybe five minutes before I got back in my chair.

The last time I did it I was working with a different artist who performs suspension. Two piercings in my back. She set up the rig and I grabbed the rope. Something about pulling the rope myself seemed challenging so I decided to do it. And I did. It felt amazing.

Those examples are fears that I can control. Situations such as I experienced with Amanda are not those I can control. There is no way to initiate those experiences. Even if there were I wouldn't want to. Having to watch that happen doesn't mean dick compared to Amanda, who was the real and only victim here. Still, I was terrified. How do you conquer that fear? How do you get over that one?

Maybe it is impossible to do so. I know I would hate to be in that situation again. But if I am, maybe having already been through it I could handle it better with someone else.

There's undoubtedly a sense of confidence when we face our fears. When we look at something that seems so terrifying and find a way to overcome it . . . I don't know. It just feels good. I think most of the things we fear we probably built up in our heads. We get stuck in our mind about a situation and feel paralyzed at the thought we will have to confront it. But when we do confront our fears and live on the other side of them we can introduce such a glorious light into our lives.

There are many people in this world who want to keep you scared. If you don't believe me just turn on the news. Many things are presented as monstrous issues or even "evil" but the reality is so few of the warnings we receive are actually worthy of true fear. I'm not saying people shouldn't be cautious because to suggest that would be irresponsible on my part. Living outside of fear, living with the confidence I have to battle these situations that cause me to be frightened or anxious has proved to be a huge, beneficial factor in my life.

Is this stance on fear a result of my philosophical interests? I think so. I was never afraid of looking at anything. For better or worse, you can tell me a hundred times to stay away from something but if I don't want to, I won't. Could be Satanism, Luciferianism, drugs, guns (my parents hated guns—brother is a sniper in the military, brother-in-law is a cop, I also partake in the pew-pew), whatever. If the interest is there, I'm probably going to dive in. There never was a fear attached to researching the occult. There was never a fear attached to the few supernatural experiences I've had. It just was. I guess I've always had the attitude of, 'the worst that can happen is death.'

One of the many lessons of my amputations was death can happen at any time, with any situation. To live in fear of that event seems silly to me. I'm significantly more cautious today than I was in my younger years, but it isn't influenced by the fear of death.

It's pain avoidance. I'm 33 and everything already hurts.

Fear initiates our fight or flight We get scared, we react. In self-defense they say you revert back to your lowest level of training. But it applies everywhere.

Perhaps my love of fear is just that . . . forcing myself to figure out the training I need to acquire. Figuring out what to do when shit hits the fan. Knowing the proper response and being prepared to effectively battle whatever it is that is making me so afraid, whether it is a gun, or an abusive husband.

CHAPTER NINE

CURIOSITY

"Whoever is delighted in solitude is either a wild beast, or a god."

—ARISTOTLE

CURIOSITY IS THE REASON FOR HUMAN EXPLORATION. Without curiosity there is no religion, no scientific discovery, no further thought as to what is—and what might be. Curiosity is the impetus for humans to extend ourselves and try to understand what we do not. Which is why curiosity is the basis for religion.

Being naturally curious is a commonality among all of those involved in the Left Hand Path. Isn't that why we jump into the occult studies in the first place?

"Oh! Look! It's dark, and dangerous, and challenging, and a solo journey? Sign me up!"

We're a weird bunch.

As each of us strives to reach our apotheosis we have to ask the questions that others cannot, or have not, found a reasonable explanation for. If Luciferians didn't piece together the various characters we base our philosophy on, it would be lost to all of us. We can easily talk about the connection between Lucifer, Prometheus, and the Nephilim (to review, it's Azazel. His story mirrors that of Prometheus in many ways. Lucifer, too.).

We can call into question our philosophical practices because before we accepted them as our own we inquired about why they existed in the first place and what their purpose was. Hermeticism and its importance to Luciferianism come into play here. But I think that questioning stems from curiosity.

An old professor explained how he thinks organized religion started. I think he is pretty close . . .

Two hunters are out one day. They are searching for a wild boar to bring back to their tribe. They find one and kill it with extreme precision. While picking the carcass up, one of the hunters notices a rock on the ground with a specific shape to it. It looks like a boar. He thinks to himself how interesting it is that he killed a wild pig and it died by a rock that looks so similar. He picks up the carcass with his tribesman and goes home.

The next day they are back out looking for another boar. No luck. The hunter who noticed the rock the day before is searching for another one. *Was it a symbol?* he thinks to himself. This time he sees no such rock. The two hunters go home without food. They are ashamed of themselves. They failed their tribe.

The following day they're out hunting again. They need food to help their tribe survive. Shortly after they venture out they find a boar. Immediately they kill it. The hunter looks around for another rock that looks like the animal. No such thing exists. He picks up the dead beast with the other huntsman and looks at the sky. There he sees a cloud that looks like a boar. He drops the carcass, which startles his companion.

He points to the cloud and asks what the other hunter sees. The tribesman says he doesn't see anything at all. The hunter says to look harder and notice how the cloud looks like a boar. The tribesman says it does not. The hunter says to look harder and explains about the rock he found the other day, and how the day they didn't find a boar they was no accompanying symbol. The tribesman looks back up at the cloud and tells the hunter that it does look like a wild boar, now that he thinks about.

Now they create symbols of boars and wear them around their necks when they go hunting. But as they do not always find their intended prey now they have to find another explanation—an excuse. Perhaps they haven't given the symbols enough attention? This is how rituals began. This is how prayer begun. All with an odd-looking rock found at the perfect moment close to a much-needed dead animal.

The curiosity of the hunter as to why he saw boar-like symbols on the days he killed a matching animal and none on the day he didn't kill a boar explains how religion started. The hunter's confusion when he didn't get his kill is highly significant. Without the sign there was no prey to kill. With the signs there was.

Why do we explore? Why do we query the world around us? Why do we quest beyond what we know? It's because we question what else there might be. We question because we are curious.

For hundreds of year scientific discoveries were made only to be shot down by the authorities—in other words, the Christian church. Their reason wasn't that the science was entirely wrong, or wrong at all for that matter, the reason was because the answer wasn't their God.

We're pretty good at believing our own bullshit. We all know the answers. We know them and if you disagree, well, you just haven't found the right answer yet. We're right. You're wrong. Our confusion—manifesting as curiosity—isn't satisfied. Nor will it ever be satisfied. Not until the answer is the answer we expect.

Everyone I know, myself included, has tried to explain an absolute fact to someone who is positive the fact is false. When we are in this situation one of two things happen. Either they accept they are wrong and change their reasoning. Or they deny it and call you an idiot for not believing their version of the "truth." We've all also been on the other side of this. Arrogance lives in all of us. Best to recognize this.

What role does curiosity play in this scenario of denial?

Curiosity is the precursor to confusion or denial. Curiosity is, once again, why we ask questions. A lack of understanding, ignorance, and an inability to understand the possibilities of what we do not comprehend are all the reverse of the open-minded seeker.

More often the follow up to confusion is denial.

Curiosity hasn't always led me to a good place. It's usually with people, not things or concepts. I am the type of person who if I do not know the answer I research the relevant subject until I do. If the answer is not readily available I will either give up or continue to research it, sometimes compulsively.

Studying years of self-defense training taught me a variety of concepts and skills. Not all training takes place in a firing range or on the mat. A lot of what self-defense training will teach you is about your mind-set. One of these mind-set concepts is to have a reason and purpose for everything you do (a point-of-view taken directly from stoic thought). I do my best to have a thought-out reason and purpose for my ideas and actions. I regularly question what I am doing and the beliefs I hold. I see this as massively beneficial because it solidifies my thoughts and actions. The issue here is—as I've come to learn throughout the years—not everyone does the same. When I question the thoughts of actions of people who have not thought intently about what they are doing or believing, they tend to get annoyed.

I understand they don't need to explain themselves to me but I'm just trying to understand their reasoning.

The one thing I have the hardest time grasping, the thing I am most curious about, is human reaction. Sometimes even my own. I had an old partner who was in school for nursing. I asked her one day why she chose nursing above all other professions. She said simply that she wanted to help people. That answer didn't add up for me. Every profession in the world helps someone, somewhere. I decided to pry ask why she wanted to help people through medicine and not another means, such as helping people buy a car. I didn't mean to sound like a smart-ass, I was trying to highlight that you can help people in a multitude of ways. Why did she choose that specific way? I was genuinely trying to understand but my questions soon offended her. We didn't see each other much after that.

Curiosity gets interesting when you start gambling with it. I had an old friend that I used to explain this kind of stuff to. He and I would talk about how we would test people, typically with small loans. We would discuss how playing stupid with someone lets you see if they are going to be honest with you. How it was always better to do this with a couple hundred before you loan them a couple thousand. Under certain conditions I'll give someone the rope to rip me off with a small loan. If they forget come pay day, I know the type of person they are. I am still selective in who I decide to test in this way but if I need to know how they are, if I need to gauge their morality, this is usually a good way to do it.

Even if I get burned in that circumstance I am still curious. Even when the answer is right there in front of me I still cannot understand why it's the way it is: If someone rips you off they simply do not care about respecting you. People know not to takes loans if they cannot pay it back. This isn't a difficult concept to understand. When someone gives you their word that they will return your money, or any other property of yours, and they don't, it's simply because they do not care.

I've dealt with this endlessly with work. From equipment borrowed and never returned, to favors that never see a ROI, it never ends. And more often than not, those same people think time causes memory loss. They almost always come back for more. At this point the only thing you owe them is a middle finger. Use it graciously.

The lack of decency is incomprehensible to me. I was raised to never go to bed owing anyone anything. My most committed Satanic sin rears its ugly head again; solipsism, the belief that others will act like you do. It's considered a sin because it means the practitioner is forgetting he/she is a unique individual who is separate from the herd (comformity).

Not all curiosity needs to be overanalyzed or even fully understood. I am curious about a lot of things. Physics is a hard subject for me to grasp. I have tried many times to understand different theories but came up blank, usually with more curiosity than when I set out to discover what I wanted to discover. But my curiosity about physics isn't one that I feel a need to absolutely understand. Someone else has dedicated his or her life to understanding it. It's not a necessity for me to become Albert Einstein or Stephen Hawking.

To be fair it's not a necessity for me to understand other peoples' actions either, but it doesn't mean curiosity won't pop up.

Sometimes the answer to your curiosity is in the absence of reaction. Human reactions confuse me all the time but sometimes it is—paradoxically—the very lack of reaction that will answer your questions. Just like my situation when loaning people money, their failure to repay me actually clarifies my curiosity. They didn't forget, they didn't care. A lack of reaction is in itself a reaction.

Went out on a date? Did it go well? Oh, it did? Then why won't they return your calls or texts? Because to them it didn't go well. Somewhere in your experience with them something put them off. And even if it isn't the answer we expect, or feel we deserve, it is still a valid response in its own way. And ultimately, it is the only one you need.

Went to a job interview? Did you answer all of their questions perfectly? Did you dress the part, look the part and spoke like you had the job? Then why didn't you get a call back? The answer to your curiosity is in the lack of response. Someone else was more qualified or your simply weren't the person they were looking for.

I absolutely understand the urge to want to know more. I am a sponge for information. Sometimes I love the answer, sometimes not. Regardless, my curious state has ended. My thirst for understanding is fulfilled, even if it leaves a bad taste in my mouth. I absolutely refuse to stop asking questions, should I feel a question is justified. More often than not if you stop talking and listen you can answer a lot of the questions you have about a situation with an individual. There is no harm in speaking up when something doesn't make sense to you.

That old saying that there are no stupid questions is incorrect—there absolutely are. But what makes the question stupid is when it hasn't been adequately researched. Be diligent first, research what you need to, or simply actively listen to the other person, then ask questions.

I have found that under most circumstances confusion is best resolved in solitude. It offers us the comfort we need and the space to not be distracted. Offer yourself a solid moment, minute, hour or day of complete solitude. Watch your life unveil before you. Watch yourself figure out these big conundrums and gain a new perspective. Watch yourself come to realize just what types of people your surround yourself with. Watch yourself end your confusion. Watch yourself evolve into this new person, even if the change is small and usually it is.

Curiosity can exist because we don't accept the reality, as mentioned earlier. Curiosity exists because we don't know the reality. Reality is not as fluid as most people believe. Sometimes facts are facts. Not everything falls into a shade of gray. It is undeniable that the earth rotates around the sun, yet for hundreds of years scientists offered this explanation but the church shot it down because they thought the universe rotated around them. There was no other explanation. Eventually the truth came out. While we have science to thank for that I don't think the majority of people's curiosity stems from scientific answers. The majority of our curiosity is related to why people do the things they do.

Enter solitude. Enter a world without distractions. Enter a world where the only things that exist are you and your thoughts. Just be careful not to stay there too long. Go dig, find your perspective, find your answers, and move on. I know if I stay there too long I will come to love myself and my thoughts so much I won't want anyone to intrude on them. I fell into this for a while. I got to the point I didn't want to be burdened by any kind of confusion. Seeing as I was so bemused by people and what and why they acted as they did, I didn't want people in my life. I'm happy to report this didn't last long, though it took a while to escape from that mind-set even after I reentered the busy everyday world.

Don't let your curiosity scare you. Don't let it run your life. At then end of the day you are responsible for yourself and only yourself. That old saying, "you can lead a horse to water but you can't make it drink" applies to much that we experience. If you are a parent you can show your children the dangers of the world. You can teach them how to navigate through them the best they can. But if they fuck up, and they will, don't let it destroy you or your opinion of them. Just as you regularly make mistakes and figure out your own life, so will they. Don't let their reactions confuse you to the point you can't look past them. Confusion isn't a substitute for action. If you have a kid and they fuck up, discipline them as you see best, try to understand their position if you can and move on.

It is in that final part that we excel ourselves. The "move on" is where we react to the answers we are given. This is entirely under your control. You have found your answer. Or maybe you haven't. But just how much will you obsess over it? How much will you let it run your life? How much will you let it rattle your brain? Hopefully only as much as you absolutely need to.

Sneak into solitude and figure it out and then sneak right back out. Even if the curiosity—your visceral bafflement—still exists, you have gained perspective. Sometimes that's all we can really gain. Perhaps the situation to the big questions behind our curiosity is not to have an answer at all. Maybe some things are just meant to be obscured, literally "occult," a secret. The same way I do things that might not make sense to observers, and sometimes they don't even make sense to me, I do them for a particular reason in that moment. Spontaneity, while fun, is usually not my style. That doesn't mean that I won't ever appear careless or reckless. It is my actions that might inspire confusion in those around me. So who I am to say the same doesn't apply for them? Chance are it does.

I don't believe people do things without a reason. Everyone reacts from the deep seat of their emotions. Even when they seem careless, or irresponsible, or stupid, they are doing it all for a reason. Sure it will confuse us. The same way we might bewilder them. But out responsibility isn't to answer all of their questions. Our responsibility is to ourselves and to justify our actions with our morality.

People will violate their own moral code to justify their current wants and needs. At the end of the day humans are basically animals. If nothing else, Satanism has taught me this because the philosophy is much more hedonistic than Luciferianism. Reminding myself of this answers many questions I have about ourselves and those around us. We all fail ourselves at some point. It is because of these failures that others usually question our actions. Their curious state builds up, understandably, because of our deeds.

Maybe I painted curiosity too darkly but it is in that state of mind that we discover and are inspired to research answers to questions that might initially seem beyond us. So ultimately curiosity can often be a beautiful thing in and of itself. It is during the complicated process of resolution that we can become disgruntled. Tread carefully.

Eve's curiosity drove her to betray the Demiurge. The argument against this would be that the serpent manipulated her. Not wrong necessarily, but if I am human so is she. If I am responsible for myself, so is she. Meaning, the motivation behind her decision to eat the forbidden fruit was a factor driven by curiosity—and furthermore, her ego.

It all starts with a question. Typically, "why?"

In Eve's case, I'd like to think it was, "why not?"

*As a side note, I'd like to offer this **theory** on Eve.

Eve was the first *human* to disobey the word of "God." Making her the first human *rebel*. The first *adversary*. The first *Satan*.

And that would make Adam the first *Satanist*, following in his wives' path to eat from the Tree of Knowledge.

"Satan" was a name given to the Babylonian King who held Jews as slaves. Judaism gave him the name of "Satan" (the adversary) to criticize him for captivating the chosen people of God (Jehovah). While Satan is typically taken to mean the opposite to God, on a supernatural, and angelic level, it was technically still a title given to a human who opposed Jehovah's chosen people, and further, Jehovah Himself.

If that title still holds the same meaning centuries prior (to the Judaic religion), Eve is also Satan. In fact, she would have been the first.

When looking at this from a Gnostic view this holds true. As Eve would have still been the first human to disobey the word of the Demiurge, represented as Jehovah, the oppressive God under the Monad.

CHAPTER TEN

DEATH

*"You will exceed them all. For you will
sacrifice the man who clothes me."*

—Jesus Christ
Gospel of Judas

I HAVE THE SAME TAKE on death as atheists . . . it's going to happen, stop worrying about it. Life is sweeter as far as I know so why spend any time thinking about death?

"What do you think happens when you die?"

Say you have spent your entire life putting the majority of your energy into your job as a marine environmentalist. You went to school, got a job, worked your ass off ensuring that the oceans were clean and the animals that live in the ocean were healthy and so on. Anyway, at some point, you will die.

I think of it like this: you've always put all your energy into oceans and water so when you die that is where your energy will go. You will become part of the oceans' current. A sort of reincarnation but on an energetic level. Energy is neither created nor destroyed so it makes sense to me that when you die you will become a part of what you put your energy toward. You will not be conscious. You will not think like you do now. But you will be a part of the oceans' current. You will be a part of the animals that live in the water. You will be a part of the energy in the water.

Imagine you have a bathtub filled with water and a dropper filled with red food coloring. The bathtub and water represent what you are putting your energy toward, in this example, the ocean. The dripper represents how you change the bathtub's water. And the red food coloring represents your energy. So, one drop of food coloring into a bathtub isn't going to change it. It still makes an effect, ripples from the drop, an extremely slight change in the water's color, but overall one drop isn't going to do anything. What if that dropper continued for years? Say, 20 years? Well, the constant ripple effect will eventually stop but the color will be changed quite significantly. Even though you are not causing the ripple anymore your energy is still paramount to the change of the bathtub.

I think that is kind of a perfect heaven too. Christians always talk about living a life that will get them into heaven but they never talk about what happens once you get there.

"YOU GET TO LIVE AROUND GOD, THE CREATOR!"

Yeah. Cool. And then what? An eternity of sitting next to a guy who makes life and takes it away? Honestly, sounds kind of boring. I think I'll pass. Put my energy toward a concert. I'd rather live in that environment for eternity than somewhere in the clouds.

Thinking this way really changes what you put your energy into. If you are consistently a part of something you don't like or appreciate then that is where you will remain when you die. Your energy there will be as unsatisfied as you are. Or maybe not. Maybe you will change your life and start living fully for yourself. Wouldn't it be better to have a life filled with purpose and when you die you remain a part of that purpose? Ayn Rand and objectivism come into play here.

On October 17, 2017, I was on my way back to Florida from California, where I got more tattoo work done. At the start of that seven-hour journey I learned some unfortunate news. My maternal grandfather was being taken to a hospice. My mom texted: "He's near death." I haven't seen him in months. I will never see him again.

It's not that I don't want to see my grandfather, it's just that I don't want to see this half-life version of him on his deathbed. He is unable to talk, hardly coherent, very disoriented and the exact opposite of who he was before he got sick. The last time I saw him he was sick but he was laughing and joking. The stroke he had caused him to sort of scramble some words but nonetheless he seemed basically okay. Typical grandpa. Making jokes at my mom's expense and us guys laughing about it. That was the last time I saw him and that's how I will remember him.

I remember around Christmas the previous year, which is when he got sick. I immediately went to the hospital to see him. My grandpa was a short, round-bellied, traditional Italian man. Lying in his hospital bed, he looked heartbreakingly frail and weak. His skin was blotchy and he had what looked like liver spots all over. My brother-in-law and my sister were in the room when I got in there. When I first saw my grandpa, I was speechless. I didn't want to tear up or cry so I kept my cool, grabbed his hand and let him talk to me for a bit.

As I found out later while smoking with my brother-in-law outside, my grandpa had a brain tumor. Inoperable. He was given anywhere from a couple of days to a couple of months. I know, when I think logically, doctors and their usual line of "they have X amount of time" is usually just to save their ass. But when I first heard that I didn't think it was bullshit. I was focused on the idea of not seeing my grandpa around much longer.

To give you some background: My grandfather immigrated from Calabria, Italy to Boston when he was in his early 20s. Then he moved to Detroit to work in the Ford factories. He was a very proud Italian

American. "I go to work every day, punch in, punch out, go home, provide for my family." Nothing wrong with that and I always admired his work ethic. He was a union man and retired after decades of hard work with a good pension.

Most of all, my grandpa was the life of the party.

He was the first to hit on some lone lady in the room and pull her onto the dance floor to boogie. She had better watch his hands too, I've seen them slide down more than once in my life. He was married for 30 years or so to my grandma but they divorced and went their separate ways when I was a kid. It seemed like he blossomed from then on. Went from "hard-working factory man" to "let me get that ass young lady." I never blamed him. I'd do the same.

He moved from Michigan to Florida when the truck hit me. Said he wanted to be closer to my mom, sister, and me (my brother was in college out of state). He remained in Florida the rest of his life. He considered moving to other states a couple of years ago, chasing tail, but ultimately decided not to.

When I got the news that terrible day I wondered if he ever thought about his own death. As a Luciferian it is a necessity in my philosophical views. Looking at the grand scheme of our lives is massively important for us, and wondering what form our pinnacle in life—what we call our "apotheosis"—will take is essential. To say we have reached our apotheosis is to say that we have become all that we can become. It stretches far beyond what we want to be remembered for, which I am sure most people think about in their old age. Apotheosis encompasses that as well, sure, but it is more of a high point that, even in death, we maintain. So the only people I can look at and judge whether or not they had ever considered the nature of their eventual Godhood are other Luciferians. It is an important part of our philosophy. It's like a Christian considering how they can live their life walking alongside Christ.

Like I said, it isn't really my place to speculate on what my grandfather's apotheosis would look like. I don't know what he would want it to be. I'm sure he thought about how he would be remembered but as mentioned above, apotheosis is much more than that. Regardless, he lived a life full of laughter and love for his family and friends. Whether or not his apotheosis was reached is irrelevant to me—I'll still remember him fondly.

On October 23, 2017, my grandpa left this world. I'll miss him dearly. He wasn't the same the last year he lived. He had many moments of lucidity and being his old self but the moments where his sickness took over were ugly, and cold, and completely unlike him. I don't give my mother, her husband, and other family members that were there enough credit for how hard that must have been on them to stay with him over the past year. I remember being with my dad in his last couple of months. I was living with him pretty much full-time. I watched him deteriorate and I too felt his life slip away. It was heartbreaking. I'm sure my mom felt the same way.

My dad died when I was 16 from cancer. Like my grandpa, it took about a year to take his life. He smoked two packs of cigarettes every day since he was 13 and eventually it killed him. This was always strange to me. My dad lived the sort of same reckless life as I adopted for so many years. He was the only man I have ever known to be legitmately fearless. Or at least that was the hat he wore, but he wore it a little too well for me not to believe it. Didn't matter how big, or how many, or what the consequences were, if you fucked with him you were getting your ass handed to you. It was like nothing could hurt him. Like he was a titan.

He wasn't just a fighter. He had a big heart. I always thought that we shared the principle of love hard, hate hard. And man, did he love. From all of his friends and family, to his six fiancées before my mom—and whoever came after her. They separated when I was 10 and divorced when I was 14. Ten years of marriage and my dad adopted my brother and had my sister and me. My mom had my brother from her first marriage. He loved us equally but differently. As he taught me, you just treat your daughters differently than your sons. With a son, you teach them to be a man. With a daughter, the opposite.

So much of what I consider a man to be comes from him. Being a man isn't about being the loudest person in the room. Or the one flashing their cash around to impress people. Or the one who needs to fight every person over every small injustice. Being a man is about being the strongest person in the background, and if you are in the spotlight, you do it with class and a certain elegance that is universally undeniable. Because he had that certain unique way about him, people respected him for it. He handled his business privately and partied with his friends openly.

Just like my grandpa, I wonder if he considered something like apotheosis. He was like a king when he was growing up and that stayed with him into adulthood. Our move to Florida never diminished his reputation in Michigan but he didn't have the same respect in our new state simply because he was a newcomer. He struggled in Florida to come to terms with that reality. I know it bothered him. It was different here. In Detroit (where he was born) people had a certain way about them. They were different. All the same I think he enjoyed bringing a piece of Detroit to the Sunshine State. As an adult I see the difference he spoke to me about. This state has far too many country clubs for him. Go ahead, treat him like you were better than him and he would've sent you a "get well" card in the hospital.

Though, when he left Michigan for Florida the hard truth is that he left behind years of established honor. He had to start over in many ways. Then, he and his wife of ten years split. Then, he and my brother stopped talking for many years. Then, a dump truck hit his son. Then, my sister had some serious issues. Life threw so many challenges at him.

After he moved he wanted his life to slow down a bit. His perspective and goals in life started to shift to another gear. He always put his kids first but without the distraction from his friends and family up north he was able to be more attentive to us. Just to raise us and provide for us seemed to become his new goal and he was satisfied with that.

My top and his top are entirely different. I have goals that exceed my father's, my grandpa's too. Doesn't make mine better, just means that I will fly higher in some respects. For example, my grandpa was a pretty funny man. He had no issues making people laugh. I, on the other hand, am not a particularly funny person. If you asked me to come up with an amusing story, chances are it would make me laugh but not you. So in that regard I do not fly higher. I just mean that I have certain aspirations that exceed what my grandpa's and my dad's were. I want the successful enterprise. I want the wealth. I want to leave a legacy. They didn't seem to care for that kind of stuff.

Death isn't something that is planned. It just happens to us. We can rarely control it. But sometimes we can.

In my freshman year of high school I had a science class where I met four great friends that I remained close to throughout school. One of them in particular I remained close to far beyond graduation. His name was Keyleigh James.

Keyleigh was one of my greatest friends ever. He and I got into quite a bit of trouble together. We had a whole crew we ran with and it was rare you would find one of us without the other. Sex, drugs, and rock and roll were our lives growing up and we indulged in every single one of them as much as possible.

When I left my hometown and moved across the state there was never a long period where Keyleigh and I didn't keep in contact. I would drive back regularly and see him and it was always like I never left. Admittedly, I pushed him many times to party when he had other responsibilities to take care of, but he did, and we always had a great time. Even when we got in trouble we would still laugh about it, sometimes years later. After a while, our stories started to blend. Too much booze and dope to remember everything individually. Regardless, I always appreciated us hanging out.

On November 8, 2017, Keyleigh took his own life. I had just spoken to him a week before and helped him out with something. All was good as far as I could see. He was excited about a new job, new volunteer company he was working with, new love interest. Everything was good, or so it seemed.

When I think about it the problems were always there. I'm not going to air out his laundry but there were many signs that all of us, his friends and family, had tragically missed. That might be the worst part. That we didn't recognize the signs and throw him the life raft that he needed. It's easy to get distracted. It's easy to miss the call for help. It's easy to look at your friend you've known for years, partied with for years, talked to for years, and see them in the light you always wanted to see them in, without recognizing the darkness that surrounds them. While I still tear up when I think about him and the town I grew up in will never be the same again, I remember my friend and the good times we had. I remember our bond. I remember him as the brother he was to me.

Keyleigh was by far the smartest friend I ever had. I know giants in the entertainment industry, finance industry, self-defense industry, and Keyleigh's intellect walked all over them. He was beyond book smart. He was witty and had an immense amount of common sense and street smarts. Keyleigh, even though he was regarded as a great friend, even though he was someone many people trusted with their deepest secrets, myself included, never reached his full potential.

I guess when I look at it and judge, it comes down to someone's capabilities. Each person has a massive amount. Unfortunately most people don't ever even so much as find theirs. You can work your entire life as a lawyer. You're good. You study, you work hard for your clients, you fight for them. But in reality, you would be a far better professional boxer. You took a couple of classes and dominated the sport. Somewhere along the way though you cared more about the "this is what you're *supposed* to do" attitude than focusing on what you are really good at. You became discouraged. You stopped going to boxing classes. You turned to law. You are still a good lawyer, but you would have been a Floyd Mayweather-level fighter.

While I have seen a lot of success in business, friendships, and family, I haven't even scratched the surface of what I know I am capable of accomplishing. Do I think that I have it in me to be the next Elon Musk? No. But do I think I have it in me to be the next John Reese or Kevin Lyman? Yes. (When I wrote this, I was still in the music industry and John Reese and Kevin Lyman put together massive touring festivals, which was a career goal of mine.)

Of course time plays a role. If I died today could I measure my apotheosis based on the time I was given? That would be hard, considering what I am capable of, but that doesn't diminish what I have already accomplished. Life is the longest thing we will ever experience but not all of it will be equally valuable regardless of how long we get.

If I died today, I would have many surface regrets. I could have promoted my last show better. I could have been a better son and brother. I could have played with my dog more. I could have, I could have, I could have . . .

Hindsight is a motherfucker. It is all too easy to fall into a negative spiral, to look at your life and say you could have done this or that differently. It is easy to forget the last time someone called on you and you selflessly gave him or her a hand, for no other reason than you love and respect them. It is easy to beat yourself up about how you could have been smarter with work, or used your time more efficiently to reach your goal. It is much harder to honestly look at yourself and know the following to be true—

'In the moment, given the tools I had, I responded to the circumstance as I best could have. I acted the way I did because it made sense at that time. In those actions I acted with integrity and honor, valuing the ideals and ethos I have chosen to adopt throughout my life. Any legacy I leave behind will be judged off that and nothing else.'

I want to be remembered as someone who lived as an example of the philosophical paths I follow. This way, when death comes creeping, you can look back and say that you lived your life fully, with purpose and intent.

Just as Rand would want. And Crowley. And LaVey. Blavatsky. Hermes Trismegistus. Jesus Christ. Buddha. Prometheus. Azazel.

All of them are relevant in my thoughts around death because each of them plays a role in how I live my life.

CHAPTER ELEVEN

BATTLING MY EGO

"A man's ego is the fountainhead of human progress."

—Ayn Rand

THIS IS ABOUT THE NUMBER ONE ENEMY of mankind—the ego.

Having an ego isn't an issue. We all have one and it is the connection between the subconscious and conscious mind that helps us determine our reality. It's a necessity for every conscious being. But having an unjustifiably unfounded inflated ego is where a necessary behavior is taken too far.

My ego-driven behavior has taken me to a variety of destinations. Some good. Far more bad. Arrogance exists in all of us, whether or not we recognize it as such. Our good intentions escape us as we inevitably slam ourselves against the walls of life. Life doesn't care about what you intended; it cares about what you did. More often than not our failures are driven by an egotistical nature that is often unfounded in reality.

Perhaps that's too vague. Here's a story as illustration:

In early 2016 I embarked on my first big project with my current company. Being a naïve newbie in the music industry, I decided to book and promote a 12-show tour with a three-band (all low-level) tour package.

If you're not familiar with the ins and outs of the touring music industry, allow me to break it down. I set up 12 concerts in five different states. That means I rented each venue and booked every band for the show (an average of five or six for each show including the three-band tour package; the rest was local support). I hired a graphics artist to design each flyer. I hired a woman named Cara to assist me. I set up financials for my company. I put up all the money for bands and venues and sent out advance tickets for the local opening bands to sell. I oversaw every part of that tour from start to finish and was hands-on in every aspect. I initiated this process only eight weeks out from the start of the tour, at the beginning of February. My company was officially started the previous November. Just four months in, the industry and I took on this kind of project!

If you are in the music industry and reading this, you're probably shaking your head. True, I have lost more money on other ventures, but this is among my most naïve, shortsighted, and dumbest business moves.

I was massively under-prepared and under-staffed for this kind of thing. On top of that I thought if a band tours a lot that means they'll automatically draw good audiences in different markets (cities). That couldn't be further from the truth. The only cities I had regularly worked in at this point were Orlando and Fort Lauderdale/Miami. I was venturing into entirely new markets blind, with no knowledge of which venues were best or which locals were the better openers.

I've owned a good number of companies over the years. None of them were music or entertainment related—one pizzeria and a couple different investment-based businesses. I am a hard worker. I typically like the act of working because it gives me purpose. I've had amazing returns on my investments with some of my companies. This isn't to say I haven't lost before, because I definitely have, and I've failed hard. Regardless, with my background I naturally figured my venture into the music industry would be similar. I have always been optimistic about my work. Why should this be any different?

Because it was entirely different. Unlike anything I ever did before.

Still, that tour gave me a hard smack that I certainly wasn't expecting.

At the start of planning it, I was exceptionally determined. I admire guys like John Reese (Mayhem Fest), Danny Wimmer (Welcome To Rockville, Carolina Rebellion), and Kevin Lyman (Warped Tour). I want the huge touring music festival featuring 20+ bands like they had. So naturally when this opportunity arose I thought to myself, *I guess this is step one.*

And yes, I am now aware that none of my heroes do what I tried to do. They might oversee the production but they don't mount those projects unless they have backing from companies like AEG or Live Nation. Plus, they are staffed with huge interactive teams.

Even when starting the planning process, I was already all in. I was working 16- to 20-hour days trying to get this tour set up. The hardest part was booking the venues. Before you can book local bands or openers for a show you need to lock in the venue.

I did 12 shows, so 12 different venues, but I probably reached out to 200. That was the first issue I ran into. Ninety percent of those venues didn't get back to me. It didn't undermine my motivation but it certainly changed my mindset toward the industry. I thought the C-list tour package I had was a great opportunity for these venues. One was signed to an indie label owned by an old A-lister in the hardcore genre. Another toured 10 months out of the year. The other was a favored client but still a small, local act. I thought I was offering these venues the best shows they could get. The reality is that I was pitching a D/C-list package.

I ended up finalizing the last venue about a week prior to the start of the tour date. With only eight weeks to plan I was impressed with my accomplishments, but at the same time I was starting to get burned out. Everywhere I looked I was hitting a wall. The tour from start to finish was only two weeks long. It involved significantly more work than I originally anticipated. The intensity didn't deter me but the small failures were starting to pile up fast. I often wondered if I was doing the right thing. Because of this I must have changed my strategy two or three times.

Next was finding bands for each market. This was a little easier because every market we were hitting was a larger city. Still, I ran into issues. Bands would jump on and immediately jump off. Bands would bitch about ticket sales. Bands would bitch about the design (or lack of) on the advanced tickets. Bands would bitch about me not getting schedules to them quickly enough. I soon learned that in the world of music everything that goes right is on the musicians and everything that goes wrong is the background workers' fault.

Welcome to the music industry!

Cara didn't help matters. I hadn't the time to find someone who was absolutely perfect so I had to go with the best individual available. I understand now just as I did then that my company is my baby. It wasn't hers. I knew she wouldn't be as devoted to this as I would be. That wasn't much of an excuse for barely lifting a finger but, hey, I still somewhat understood. At the end of the day I was giving her experience with pay. A very small pay, true, but any money is still a motivating factor for most people. This experience gave her the opportunity to learn just as much as I was going to. I didn't hide anything from her—she had just as much access to what was going on as I did (minus some of the financial details).

The work I did for this tour was among the hardest I have ever worked on a business project. I was so driven by my goals that even with the walls I was hitting, I still had that amazing confidence in my abilities. I really thought I was the shit for doing this. No one else was doing what I was doing. While that should have been a warning to me, it turned out to be a motivating factor. I thought I was standing out from the crowd for doing this tour. Like this alone would boost my name.

Still, come time for me to leave home and go on tour, I was tired. I was also starting to get confused. Fortunately I wrote literally everything down and kept my organization in pristine condition. If I hadn't, I would have made even more mistakes. In my head, the North Carolina show was blending with the Jacksonville show, which was blending with the Gainesville show, and so on. It all started to look the same.

The day of the first show arrived. Cara and I were the first ones there, but not long after, the bands showed up. The venue owner opened up for us and we went inside.

One of the determining factors when you book a show is the venue capacity. You don't want to book a stadium for a show that will only attract a thousand, and you don't want to book a 50-capacity venue for a show that will bring out 500. The minute I saw this space I felt defeated. I had expected a large room with roughly 150 capacity. I got an empty basement with no stage.

My head started to spin but I still had work to do. No time to think about anything else. Load the bands in. Make sure the merchandise is set up. Sound check.

The fucking sound technician left before the show for about an hour for unknown reasons. Most venues provide a sound technician and because of that, I hadn't arranged a backup. Fortunately, the headliners' tour manager handled the sound till he returned.

I don't know why I was so worried about capacity, seeing as the first act was the only one to actually draw people. At the beginning it looked decently full, but I knew whether it's packed out or empty, you can't judge a whole show on how many heads are in the door for the first band.

I had high hopes for the headliner because that city happened to be where their label was based. Definitely not what I was expecting, but they did okay.

I lost big on that show. Not the best way to start off the tour.

While driving to the next venue I felt deflated. I'd had exceptionally high hopes for that first show but I lost a lot of money. I still felt optimistic, but the sense that I was doing something wrong, that I had made some key mistake, started to creep up on me. No one in the tour package did anywhere near as well as I had hoped for. Still, most of the money for this tour was already paid out and the money that was not paid went to the artists, gas, per diem (daily allowance for food) for myself and Cara, and incidentals.

Regardless of whether or not the artists did well, I felt obligated to pay them. Never once throughout this entire tour did I say to myself that they didn't deserve or earn the money. In this industry, not paying an artist is one of the worst things you can do for your reputation. I didn't want to start off on a bad foot, so no matter what fee we had agreed to, it got paid. The same went for Cara. Some things you just need to take the hit on.

The next day was the Georgia show.

Something was wrong with me.

Everyone was loading in their gear and setting up their merchandise. I was directing the bands and busy with my usual routine. I felt like shit. My chest was in pain. My vision blurred. I knew this show would be like the previous one.

I went outside and paced around for a bit. I thought maybe if I got away from everyone, I could take a breather, relax for a brief moment, and get back to work. I ended up in the back of the venue. A massive feeling hit me like I was having a heart attack, with a terrible urge to vomit at the same time. My entire body's muscles contracted. I could see the veins in my arms popping out. I only managed to stay upright by planting my hands on the front of my wheelchair. That stopped me from total collapse.

In that moment, though, behind the venue in bum-fuck Georgia, I was certain I was going to die.

I never had a panic attack before. It scared me. It all happened so fast. It did take a moment for me to return to normal, but when I did, I lit a cigarette and returned to work.

That show went horribly, as expected.

That night I had to drive to Orlando for a court case (which I can't talk about for legal reasons). After court, which went the exact opposite way my lawyer had predicted, I had to ride out to Jacksonville for the next show. I arrived before any of the bands and drove to an abandoned parking lot. I sat there for an hour or so. I had been awake for 40 hours and was completely zonked out. I was depressed about the tour. Depressed about court. I just wanted to scream and cry.

That show was shit, too.

The following gig was in Daytona. My first matinee. Not only did it not bring a crowd, it was the first time in my career I almost got into a fistfight with a band member—the drummer of one of the openers. Cocky prick. I was told he was kicked out of the band after that incident. Good riddance.

I think you get the picture by now. Out of 12 shows, only three brought a crowd. Only two made money. I never wanted something for my business to work out so well and have it crash so hard.

Let's review this experience from two different egocentric philosophical standpoints.

The first, objectivism.

The most obvious point here is that an inflated ego opposes the base foundation of objectivism, meaning reality is separate from the ego and therefore decisions should be based on reality, not the ego. This is true. But at the time I didn't think I had an inflated ego that was driving this. I thought I was ambitious but still informed enough to perform my actions. Being completely new to the industry does count for something, true, but my naivety can't count for everything.

The reality I was failing to recognize was that my tour package wasn't actually big. There were plenty of signs along the way, but I ignored all of them. I felt like once I had started this I couldn't stop. I knew that going in.

I started to question around the Georgia show if I should cancel the tour. It would've been a scar on my reputation in the industry. Not one that would last but undeniably one that would've been difficult to recover from in the beginning stages of my career.

How does this balance out with the financial loss I knew was coming? I figured I would lose about $10,000 and I turned out to be pretty close. Again, terrible way to kick the business off. If I stopped halfway through the tour I could've saved another $4,000 or so.

Would it have been worth it? Through the eyes of objectivism, yes, I think so. The reality is I made a mistake. I knew that shortly after the tour started. Taking that reputation hit, if looked at realistically, wouldn't have been a death sentence. I wasn't a big enough name for anyone to notice or care. Would I have burned some bridges? Yes. Could they have been rebuilt? The important ones, yes.

For me, my word in the industry was more important than anything. While this is important, the reality was that it wasn't worth it. If I had been more business-minded with this venture instead of trying to be a man of my word, I would've made several smarter business decisions over the course of my career.

On the flip side, I gained my reputation in my industry for being transparent and straightforward. For paying bands regardless of whether or not the show did well. Integrity counts for a lot in everything I do, not just work.

Next, let's view this from a stoic lens.

In principle I believe I upheld my stoic nature throughout this process. While I understand my efforts to hide my dissatisfaction fell short, I did still complete what was within my moral frame. I made an agreement with the tour package, the venues, the local supporting acts. To pull out of this for a selfish, materialistic purpose would've been the undeniable mark on my integrity, which I have tried to maintain since I was in my early 20s.

I've been the unbearable, unsufferable, micromanaging douche boss, too. I learned my lesson at the piercing studio when I saw a variety of my actions toward employees of my pizzeria presented back to me by the ownership. Being on the receiving end of that dramatically changed my ownership and management style.

I went into business ownership thinking because I now owned a business that meant I had to be a Steve Jobs archetype; my excuse for being on a power trip and an asshole. But after I had a taste of what a dick boss is like, I swore I'd never be like that again.

Luckily by the time the music industry work rolled around, I understood a reality that is true in nearly every circumstance—*you attract more bees with honey*. When it comes to work, that is never not true. As a business owner or someone in management you need to embrace that idea. It has been proven that Machiavellianism isn't as effective in the workplace as compassion and empathy toward your coworkers.

I'll admit, when I started treating people better in the workplace it didn't come from a place of empathy; it came from my greed. I knew if my employees were happy they would work harder for me because I recognized the above statement to be true. I saw the effect it had, not just on profits but on productivity and fun in the workplace. I became quickly convinced.

On the tour I grew a massive disdain for Cara. I resented the musicians too, but only because I blamed them for my shortcomings in seeing how bad of an idea this was. My disdain turned to disrespect, and I grew more and more sick of the entire thing. Looking back, she really was a terrible employee. I also wasn't the best employer.

Is it not my job to lead and inspire my team?

As for the tour, I upheld my stoic foundation as much as I could have. Yes, my disappointment showed, but I kept my word and completed what I had to complete.

Did my ego lead me somewhere I wanted to be? No. My ambition did. My ego led me to losing an unnecessary $10,000 in the first year of my company. Something that took years to fully recover from with other new business expenses.

Did I make the smart choice as far as objectivism is concerned? No.

Did I make the smart choice as far as stoicism is concerned? I think so.

In my entire career I have never backed out of a deal with a band. I have completed and fulfilled each agreement I have made. I take a sense of pride in that, especially seeing as my industry is famous for sleazeballs.

Even still, being someone who doesn't uphold his word is a nasty reputation to shake, in work or in life. Do everything you can to avoid this.

CHAPTER TWELVE

JUDGMENT

"Satan represents responsibility to the responsible, instead of concern for psychic vampires!"

—Anton LaVey
The Satanic Bible

LUCIFER: *You stand before this court accused of crimes against yourself. How do you plead?*
ME: Not guilty!
LUCIFER: *Make your case.*
ME: Kendra and I met on a dating app. She was just looking for friends as she was already taken. We talked for hours about politics, religion, culture, music, and more. We really hit it off. Over the following weeks we continued to establish our friendship. Kendra was fun to be around and our personalities seemed to complement one another.

Kendra and her boyfriend separated, which was a long time coming from what I was told. I was attracted to her but I never tried to make a move.

SAMAEL: *And then you broke your leg.*

ME: Correct. Kendra visited me every day at the hospital. Due to previous experiences in that environment I really didn't want anyone there. It's a special kind of vulnerable to have someone see you in a hospital bed and I wasn't at that comfort level with her. She pushed through and came regardless.

LILITH: *Did that upset you at all?*

ME: At first, yes. I thought she was being pushy. But after her first visit I realized I wanted her there. She was a much needed distraction.

LUCIFER: *What happened next?*

ME: I had a freshly broken leg and I was back on painkillers so we couldn't do much. She would come over, we'd order food, watch movies, play games. About a week after I got out of the hospital I took her with me to a concert I booked. It was here we decided to give "us" a go.

Understand Kendra, at first, looked too good to be true. Instead of taking that as a warning I was a fool and thought I hit the jackpot.

SAMAEL: *You were very dedicated to this relationship from the start. You really wanted it to work. It seemed as if everything else took a backseat in your mind. Kendra moved to the forefront.*

ME: At that time, yes. So much wasn't going well for me. It seemed like one problem led to another. Breaking my leg meant I had to get back on painkillers, which meant I would have to experience the withdrawals again, not to mention stop all walking training for months. Work took a serious decline, too. So I put my energy and effort towards the sexy, foreign brunette with a nice rack bouncing in my lap.

Call me weak.

LILITH: *In your early experiences with her did anything come off as strange or abnormal?*

ME: The only thing that comes to mind was how into me she was from the start. Yes, it was flattering but it did make me wonder. She was really, *really* into me. More than any woman ever had been. It's one thing when you're spending time with them in person but with her it was 24/7 intrigued. At times I found her nonstop interest annoying.

LUCIFER: *What was the first sign of trouble?*

ME: That depends. Are you referring to the situation with her mom or her extremely unstable mental state?

LUCIFER: *Let's start with her mom.*

BELIAL: *Why did you see it as necessary to help with that? In what way was that your problem?*

ME: I had fallen in love by that point.

BELIAL: *Yes. Just under two months in.*

ME: Right. I had never been in love before. It was one of the most overwhelming emotions I have ever experienced. Kendra made me feel a way no other woman made me feel. I wanted to bring her into my life. I wanted a life that aligned with her. We both moved fast—

BELIAL: *We are here to discuss YOUR involvement! Kendra made her choices but do not think for a second that excuses you from the decisions you made. This is about YOU! Not her.*

ME: I understand.

I started to notice a shift in our relationship I really wasn't crazy about. It got to a point I couldn't joke or tease her in any way or her entire day would've been ruined. Which was weird because prior to us being a couple she had thicker skin. We would talk shit to each other regularly and neither of us took it personally. She got triggered a lot for someone who took time out of her day to troll people online as often as she did. It didn't make sense to me.

So I took her on various dates. I bought her stuff. She was a cheap date in the beginning.

LILITH: *Did you feel she desired you like you desired her?*

ME: Looking back, I don't know. Whether she was as into me romantically as I was into her or whether or not that's just what I wanted to believe, it's hard to tell the difference. I can confidently say *now* I was being played. But at the time I felt loved.

I guess she felt that I wasn't doing enough. She said I needed to show her I loved her in ways outside of the dates and gifts. Then the situation with her mom came up. First, it was her mom was coming to America from Europe to get her green card. The next issue was Kendra had access to her mother's bank account stateside. Kendra, being a full-time student, needed money at times. The account was $7,000 short of what it was supposed to be, which happened over a period of two years.

So now her mother was coming for, what I was told, three weeks to a month, max. But that meant her mom would know the account was short.

I told her I'd loan her the difference until her mom left. She was living with her ex-boyfriend and a roommate and she didn't have much space. She and her ex were always at each other's throats too. I said I'd house both her and her mom until her mom left.

LUCIFER: *How long had you two been together by the time her mom arrived?*

ME: Just over two months.

LUCIFER: *So to make sure we're all on the same page, you gave your girlfriend of two months $7,000 and offered to house her mother while she worked to get her green card?*

This was so unlike you. You've had a lot of roommates over the years—but loan thousands of dollars to someone you hardly know? It's one thing to do it for a friend who has established credit with you. But for a new partner?

BELIAL: *Captain Save-A-Ho!*

ME: I know how stupid and shortsighted this is. I'm aware. I just wanted something to go right at a time when nothing seemed to.

Back then, the idea that she was using me never ever crossed my mind, even when close friends raised concern. Even when she would show signs that she was I always brushed it off and gave her an excuse. It was naïve of me.

As for her mom, she swore up and down it was going to be a month, tops. For me to lock up $7,000, for a month at most, at that time wasn't an issue. I had a spare bedroom and bathroom. Why not?

Keep in mind I was pretty heavily medicated at this time. That has to count for something.

LILITH: *It does but don't put it on us. You knew something was off. That was our light. You ignored it. Nothing about her being in your life, after her mother arrived, made you feel better. Everything after mother arrived had become "how can Henry jump through hoops for Kendra?"*

ME: Hindsight's always 20/20.

LUCIFER: *Elaborate on your relationship after her mother arrived.*

ME: It wasn't ideal. There was definitely a change. We stopped having regular sex, she seemed like she was always stressed out and she became really irritable over small, insignificant shit.

BELIAL: *And that wasn't a sign for you to leave her? We know you thought about leaving her somewhat regularly. But you stayed. Why?*

ME: I figured her attitude was due to her mom stressing her out. It wasn't like I saw Kendra like she was at the end of our relationship right off the bat. For the first three months or so there really weren't any issues that I felt warranted a breakup. She would do things I thought were annoying or stupid, like bringing up her ex-partners regularly, but for whatever reason I didn't see that as a break-up-worthy problem. I was determined to make it work. I just kept thinking about how great it was. It's like being addicted to a drug—I was chasing that original high.

Upon this I had never really committed to a woman before. So why not now? I remember certain times when I would think about ending it and second guess myself, figuring it was a commitment issue on my end.

BELIAL: *You felt determined? As opposed to . . . love? Peace of mind? Comfort? Determination shouldn't be the leading emotional state in a new relationship. That's not how it is supposed to work and you knew that then and know it now.*

I'm really just starting to think you woke up stupid for a couple months.

ME: Can't say I disagree.

SAMAEL: *Look at you. You're finally making sense.*

ME: Right.

LUCIFER: *And her suicidal tendencies?*

ME: It seemed real. I haven't seen a lot of that behavior in my life but from what I did see, she looked like she easily could've been a threat to herself. She was aware of her depression and anxiety issues but I never thought she understood how bad she could be. All the same, there were times I think she pulled the suicide-card to get me to pay more attention.

But her depressive episodes, at least at that time, seemed very real. The two times she left my home threatening to kill herself didn't look like a joke.

LUCIFER: *What happened the last time she went through one of these episodes? The first was dropped quickly, wasn't it?*

ME: Yeah. That was so weird to me. Like a light switch. One night I was chasing her around town trying to find her. The following morning she wanted to act like nothing happened. I lost my shit that night looking for her. And she just went on like it was totally normal.

The idea that someone might threaten suicide just to fuck with their romantic partner was outside of my perspective. Looking back, I think she was trying to teach me a lesson.

The first time was triggered because I told her no and didn't let her have her way.

The second time was triggered because I called her out and said she needed to realize she was being the problem. It pushed her over the edge she was already teetering on. She was at my house and decided to leave. I let her, not knowing how she was really feeling. I called her shortly after to try and mend our relationship but was met with hostility. I couldn't understand most of what she said because she was crying so hard. In time, I convinced her to come back home.

When she came back she went straight to my room to sleep. I tried to talk to her but she immediately told me she wasn't interested. She said no one was going to say anything useful anyway. I replied with okay and went to leave the room. I figured it would be smart to give her the space she needed. On top of that I was fed up with her by this point. Every small thing was like an end of the world issue and I was sick of dealing with it.

She apologized to me and called me back. Like a lamb to slaughter, I went.

As we spoke, I remember she said she was convinced suicide was the best answer to her problems. Nothing else made sense to her. She said people would move on without her. People who she was close to would eventually smile again. People would find her replacement. As I tried to plead with her I felt I was hitting a wall with everything I said. Nothing I could say made any sense to her. She didn't want to hear it and I felt trapped.

LILITH: *Henry, there is nothing else you could've done for her. You were already doing so much.*

ME: We were only together for a total of eight months. In that time she had these episodes, as far as I knew, twice, maybe three times. I never had this experience before. I've never had someone I cared that much about—romantically, period—but then to hear them talk about wanting to die . . . It just hit me.

Keyleigh died about a week after her mother arrived. Suicide was a very real, very "this-does-actually-happen" thing for me at that time.

Looking back the two lessons are pretty obvious. First, *if you don't let me have my way, I'll threaten to kill myself.* Second, *if you have expectations of me, I'll threaten to kill myself.*

LILITH: *I think so as well. But at that time that wasn't clear to you. What did you do?*

ME: It ruined me. I pushed her to go see a therapist. Get on medication. She tried meds on and off for a little while but it was a constant uphill battle that lasted all of a week each time.

I thought I could help her. Which I think plays a big role in my actions. I understand they are still my responsibility and I'm not making an excuse but it was one of the most heartbreaking experiences I've ever endured. And I went through it twice in five months.

I just wanted to help her. All the annoyances, all of the fighting, all of the bullshit aside, I cared about her quite a bit. At some point I became her enabler.

AZAZEL: *They call this codependency.*

ME: I know. Maybe it was because she was the first love experience I had. Maybe it was because I saw it up close and personal for the first time. Maybe it's because I was dulled out on dope. But that term has never applied to me at any other point in my life. I'm the most independent person I know. I've never needed the approval of anyone to do anything. Nor did my external relationships count for the entirety of my self-worth. This situation, for whatever reason, was different.

With Kendra and this last episode, I wanted to leave her. I really did. But our discussion hooked me back in.

LUCIFER: *Why did you leave her the first time?*

ME: What reason did I have to stay?

LUCIFER: *What do you mean?*

ME: How many times could I deal with her bullshit? The situation with her mom overstaying her welcome. I was severely sick once and she did next to nothing to help. I couldn't count on her to do anything for me. I would get screamed at over any small issue, whether it involved me or not. She once insulted me repeatedly in front of my family; she took zero responsibility for herself, her life and liked to consistently remind me I was doing something wrong; there was an almost complete lack of intimacy; she was easily the most negative person I've ever met, having an endless list of crises and problems; I had extreme doubts she was being faithful—and she never shut the fuck up about previous hook-ups or past boyfriends.

It was like dating someone who has the mentality of a bratty ten-year-old with severe mental issues. Enough was enough!

I still had an emotional attachment. I might have called it love at the time but it wasn't that. It was something else. After I ended things with her I went to the bar to meet up with a friend.

My friend I met at the bar had been married twice and always wished he tried to make it work with his exes. He suggested couple's therapy.

BELIAL: *You didn't see anything wrong with being with someone for less than six months and being asked if you tried couple's therapy?*

ME: Of course I did. I didn't plan on doing it at the bar. As I drove home I remember thinking I wanted her to see a therapist, thinking that might help her. She had told me she had seen them before and it helped. Maybe this was an unexplored option worth taking.

SAMAEL: *How did therapy go?*

ME: Horribly the first time. Better the second time, until the end of the session anyway. We didn't take a third trip until weeks later.

I saw that therapy wasn't working. I didn't expect much from two sessions but it was abundantly clear to me Kendra could not take criticism. It didn't matter if I said it or the therapist said it. She absolutely could not accept that she fucked up. That she made mistakes. If she did hear us out, her response was always the same . . . *Well, I guess I'm just a piece of shit!*

AZAZEL: *Why do you think she responded in that way?*

ME: I don't know but I remember asking my therapist and she said at some point it just catches up to them. At some point they can't pretend anymore and they realize what they are really doing. Maybe she was right. Or maybe it was just another childish response from Kendra. Who knows?

Still, I tried to make it work.

I have found our arguments seemingly had more chance in my favor if they were written out so I took that approach. I wrote a list of my wants and needs and told her to do the same.

I can at least say at this point if this didn't work, I was ready for it to end.

SAMAEL: *Oh I'm sure of it! How'd it go?*

ME: She surprised me. She actually agreed with the vast majority of what I wrote. But I didn't take this opportunity as one to call her out necessarily. My "list" wasn't an insult to her.

AZAZEL: *I'm guessing hers wasn't as . . . fair?*

ME: Afraid not. I was blamed for three things that were completely outside of me and our relationship. She was hypocritical.

LUCIFER: *How?*

ME: Her mom was with us for four months. Remember, "we" expected it to be a month, max. I didn't have the heart to kick her out. Everything aside, her mother was a genuinely kind and extremely nice woman. Complete opposite of Kendra. Kendra was a Monday through Friday full time student. I work from home, where her mother stayed. She and I built a good relationship.

I wanted her to leave but I also wanted her daughter to handle it. I knew even if her mom did leave I was still going to be expected to handle it somehow. Staying with Kendra was my new life goal. So what difference did it make?

Anyway, her mom overstayed her welcome. I told her no guests after that. She conveniently forgot and she had a friend stay with us for a week. I was far beyond the push over point, I just didn't see it yet. In my head I was giving her an ability to just relax. In reality, at this point, I was borderline owned. We were still broken up and "trying to make it work." I didn't have to let her friend stay there. It was my home, my territory. Until I gave it away, mentally speaking.

LILITH: *Henry, this doesn't add up. You had multiple valid reasons to leave, and then you did, and then you tried everything you could to make it work. Why? Was it not clear to you that your relationship was done? Was it not clear she had checked out?*

ME: I realize now that the objective here was always just to make it work. Although lonely, I didn't see myself as desperate when we got together. Still don't. But I did become desperate for her over the course of our relationship.

Even then it was confusing to me. I didn't know why I was so dedicated. She clearly wasn't. Any feeling of relief when she was around was long gone.

I guess this is what they call the "trauma bond."

Her mom was gone, and with her the stress she brought along for both of us. She surprised me by agreeing to most of what I said, even if she was hypocritical in her response. For me, that was enough.

LUCIFER: *So you were together again?*

ME: For a whomping three to six weeks, depending on how you look at it.

LUCIFER: *What happened?*

ME: About three weeks after we got back together she woke up in a panic. I didn't know why until much later in the day. I just knew she woke up freaking out, asking me if I thought she was awake and then she went to sleep in the other room.

Later in the day she told me she was sure I was fingering her in her sleep.

I was awake when she woke up. My hand was on her leg, above her pajamas. Not even close to the outside of her vagina let alone inside of it. I was stunned at her accusation. I left my home for a couple hours, trying to process this new claim. This one scared me.

We didn't talk the rest of the day.

BELIAL: *Her stubbornness was incredible.*

ME: I got angry. I'm not going to get accused of sexual assault and take that lying down. Fuck that! We argued about it and she started having a panic attack, or what looked like one.

Seeing as I was her enabler for months at a time, maybe she figured I would just roll over to her every command, which in this case was her usual, "I don't want to talk about it!"

Not for this. You accuse me of something this serious, we're talking about it—"difficult conversation" or not.

LUCIFER: *What happened the next day?*

ME: I was getting ready for the gym and she came up to me and apologized for yelling. She said it was a conversation she wanted to have in front of a therapist.

AZAZEL: *When was the appointment?*

ME: Three weeks later, per Kendra's request. I told her I didn't want to wait that long. She said she wasn't willing to miss school.

Later that week she had an appointment she was willing to miss school for. Laser hair removal, which she wanted me to get her. A suggestion to fix her low sex drive.

A story as old as time . . .

As soon as she said she wasn't willing to miss school for it I knew I was done with her and our disgusting excuse for a relationship.

We had an argument about her living situation just days before this all happened. She started to move out of our bedroom, bathroom and closet. I didn't understand why and raised concern that she was distancing herself from me. She got defensive, telling me it was all in my head and I was overthinking the situation. Then, days later, she is allegedly assaulted.

Guess where she stayed after that? Guest room. Where she had already moved the majority of her stuff. The bathroom was cleared out, too.

She was very quick to repeat that line. That shit was all in my head. Everything was coincidental with her. Nothing was as it seemed. But you tell me . . . what's this look like to you?

SAMAEL: *You didn't end it there though. Why?*

ME: I saw her now. Maybe not entirely but I saw enough of the obvious picture she was painting. I figured if I dump her she will start making claims. With this accusation I came to realize there was a high possibility I wouldn't be the first guy she made this type of false claim against. One of her many stories with multiple holes finally made sense. It was extremely likely she had made a false sexual assault claim against a previous partner. If it got her what she wanted, I doubt she would think twice about going there.

She told me she accepted it might not have happened. I needed someone else to hear that. Like a licensed therapist who has seen her disgusting behavior on two separate occasions and has seen me for well over a year.

In those three weeks, I hardly said a word to her. I think she knew it was coming. She didn't care anymore because she knew I didn't care anymore. I was over it. With that came an end to her supply. So she was over it too.

LUCIFER: *You go to your therapist, she tells her end, you tell your end. Your therapist has heard her say that she accepted it might not have happened like she thought it did. That it was unlikely.*

ME: Yes. As soon as I heard that, along with her excuse for missing school for a cosmetic appointment but not this, I told her we were done for good.

SAMAEL: *What was the excuse anyway?*

ME: She had the appointment for a month.

LUCIFER: *Then what happened?*

ME: I held back to extreme urge to throw her out of the second-story window behind her and settled on kicking her out. How I held my cool is a mystery to me.

I threatened to take her to court over the remaining money she owed me. She had paid me back half but when it was discussed during my failed list attempt, I was a horrid ass for expecting her to pay me back the other half. Her friend and her got gold plated grills for their teeth while her friend was in town. She clearly had the money.

She was *fuming*. Not only was she dumped twice by someone she absolutely despised by this point, but she also just got kicked out of her home, threatened to go to court, told she has to start supporting herself, and it was made *exceptionally* clear to her I'm not listening to her bullshit anymore.

On top of all of this, it all happened with a witness. One who heard her flip her story four times in fifteen minutes and say a cosmetic appointment meant more to her then ironing out a molesting claim against her current boyfriend. She couldn't make a legal claim now that would actually go anywhere. That would never stand in court with what happened in my therapist office. And my guess is she figured that one out, too. Truthfully I was *shocked* she showed up.

I had few wins in this situation but knowing she drove home from my therapist not having an option but to do what I was telling her to do . . . warms my heart. She was an incredible control freak who clearly forgot her place in *my* home. It felt great to remind her.

LUCIFER: *Let's go to the move-out day. She was supposed to pay you a portion of the money she still owed you.*

ME: She was supposed to pay me all of it, just in installments.

LUCIFER: *What happened?*

ME: Long story short, a couple days after I broke up with her the first time she bought www.HenryPaniccia.com and tried to get me to pay $300 for it. Shortly after she bought it she told me a story about how she did this once before to someone who, she claimed, raped a friend of hers. I remember her telling me that she built a website, using this guy's first-name-last-name.com, with keywords in the background linking it to child porn.

I was furious, shaking with anger. She said she wouldn't do that to me but if that was true why bring it up in the first place? I had to leave my home before I beat her into a coma. This fucking cunt! I was still housing her mom and she pulls some shit like this on me? But what could I do? We didn't talk about it much and when we did she said she would give it to me for my birthday, months away.

I had a choice; take the $3,500 she owed me or take $600 and www.HenryPaniccia.com. If she published that website my company would suffer. Reputation counts for a lot in what I do.

I lost it. I couldn't hold it together. Emotions took complete control of me and I argued and cried for an hour with her.

It just hit me. It was the insult that felt like vinegar on a wound. It was one of her many betrayals that tore me up. It was realizing that even if I still cared for her, albeit in some small way, I meant absolutely nothing to her. It was realizing I never meant anything at all, outside of a means to an end. It was realizing I was right about her. I was used and had been for a long time. She even did me the favor of admitting that fact.

I remember her telling me if I took the $3,500 the domain would then cost $5,000 and she would publish it in a week or less, promising me it would have a damaging effect. She referenced that conversation about that other guy repeatedly throughout this one. I'm not particularly tech savvy. Her threat seemed possible if you know how to code, which she had some experience with.

It became clear that no matter what I said it wouldn't change her mind. So I took the $600 and HenryPaniccia.com. And I haven't seen her since.

AZAZEL: *As you know now, this is a partial lesson in not having attachment to things. If you had been willing to lose that money you could've had her gone LONG before you did. Was it worth it?*

ME: Absolutely not. She paid me $3,000 back relatively quick. If I had been more willing to lose the balance, so I could lose her, this situation would've been much less damaging.

LILITH: *Do you still desire her?*

ME: No. The mask started to fade before it got really bad. The extremely interesting young woman before me had a variety of holes in her stories the more she told them. A lot of the things that initially attracted me to her were lost only a couple months in. But again, I was determined.

SAMAEL: *You never once thought about boundaries in relationships. Not to say you had none but it wasn't a conscious thought. Is it now?*

ME: It is. And while I have never, in any way, had a relationship with anyone like this, there are some elements that have been repeated throughout my life. This was just an extremely magnified version.

BELIAL: *You were so determined to make it work you didn't stop to ask if you should. Do you see the issue in that?*

ME: Yes. Like I said the initial attraction didn't last beyond a couple months. It was almost competitive on my end. Like I had to win her over.

LUCIFER: *Henry Paniccia, I find you guilty of stupidity. I find you guilty of disrespecting the most important source of divinity in your life—yourself. I find you guilty of giving so much to someone who gave so little. I find you guilty of letting emotions completely dictate your actions. I find you guilty of accepting far less than you deserve. I find you guilty of entirely forgetting every philosophical ideal you hold close, because none of it is found in your actions throughout this relationship.*

Before you say Crowley's "love is the highest Law; Love under Will," this wasn't you following your will. It was you being a slave to hers.

You are absolutely not to blame for her actions. It is not your fault she did this to you. There is not a single mistake you made as a partner that warrants this kind of behavior. But you are still responsible for yourself and your actions, even when it hurts to admit it.

When you got together it seemed like the world was crashing down. You had your withdrawals, your leg broke, your grandfather and friend died during the time you were with her and much more. You credit this whirlwind of shit as the reason you stayed as long as you did. And maybe that's true. But this became painstakingly obvious so early on that she was using you. You kept denying it, again and again, and this is the result of that action.

Do you understand this judgment?

ME: I do.

LUCIFER: *I really hope you see the light here. For months you ignored every ounce of it that we shed on this situation. All of the signs were there.*

You still decided to leave. That's not easy to do. After your last withdrawal, and you stopping nearly all painkiller use, you really started to see her for who she was. The first time you left her was less than a month after your last withdrawal. What you fail to realize is that Kendra's greatest weapon against you wasn't yourself, as you have explained to your therapist. Kendra's greatest weapon was becoming the new addiction you didn't realize you had. You were able to force yourself through opiate withdrawal. This was something else entirely.

It is in our opinion that Kendra qualifies as what is called a "dark triad." We hardly can consider these people actual human beings, but it is those with a combination of cluster-B personality disorders in one. Not that it matters. Kendra was the storm. This was about how you weathered that storm.

She once told you, while she was feeling down, that she felt like she was being chased all her life by a beast. She said she was scared but also tired of running. Remember your response to her? You said nothing. You couldn't relate. There is not a single issue in your life you haven't faced head on. Not a single doubt you haven't stared down. You can and have fought every "beast" in your life. She never will. It's a tragic impossibility for her.

You were in a war you didn't realize you were in, and the vilest of enemies was someone you thought was your closest ally.

Learn to accept that—and let all of this go. It's done.

One of the main reasons I wanted to come back and do a third edit is because I can now say I'm actually healed from this. This relationship was the worst experience I've ever endured. This topped losing my legs at 11, being in a hospital for three months, my father's death, the withdrawals, everything.

I no longer hold such a harsh judgment against myself for this relationship. Lucifer's first judgment against me is that of stupidity, and I want to make it clear I no longer hold that view. But I also wanted to show that even though this book was released over three years after she left my home, I still had that view of myself in this relationship.

It took until 2023 to heal from an abusive relationship I was in for eight months during 2017 and 2018. This relationship caused me to have severe PTSD symptoms during those six years.

On the rare occasion I felt the need to explain to someone what a PTSD episode felt like, I would tell them to think of the worst non-physical fight they have ever been in. Doesn't matter with who. Remember the adrenaline. Remember the racing heartbeat. The hairs on your neck standing up. The desire to let out a mass of energy but for whatever reason, you're not able to.

Do you have an experience in mind? Good.

Now get yourself back in that physical state. I want your heart racing. I want the adrenaline going. The fight or flight is activated. You're anxious, on edge, and ready to battle.

Are you there? Good.

Now reenact the fight while facing a wall. I want the same vigor, same energy, same viciousness, but do it to your wall.

Now repeat this for hours on end.

I spent years locked in my arguments with her. Fighting demons that only existed in my mind. Ghosts in my home, which I foolishly didn't move out of for over two more years. I remember thinking I didn't want to let her win.

I hardcore isolated for years, which was the worst thing I could have done. I felt so much shame, guilt, and emasculation over this relationship it was all I could think of. It helped me make other bad choices with other relationships. It helped destroy a couple others.

JUDGMENT

It takes time to move past something like this. If you've dealt with this kind of experience, my heart goes out to you. I'm over here bitching about getting scammed for $2,900 and getting my feelings hurt. I cannot imagine what this would've been like if we had kids.

For the men and women fighting that battle, I wish you the best of luck.

If there was any lesson I learned from this experience it was this:

If you do not love and respect yourself, no one else will.

Remember that moving forward with all of your relationships and you will create a community of like-minded people you can lean on and trust to correctly guide you, should you run into this same issue. Find people you trust, who are doing well in their lives, and let them in. It's okay to be vulnerable. If I had been honest with my best friend at the time about what was happening, this would've been cut short long before it got to the point it did. It's not that I couldn't have leaned on him for this; it's that I was too ashamed of myself to admit to him that certain things were happening.

It's not that you hold no responsibility. You do, even when it hurts to admit it. I can blame lack of experience in a committed relationship, I can blame her, I can blame everything external that didn't go right at this time. That doesn't dismiss me entirely. That may seem harsh to some but it's the truth.

You are responsible for yourself, always.

Lastly, I want to note that even over three years later, I still had difficulty understanding my own codependent traits. If I didn't know you, I couldn't have cared less what your perspective was. But if I did know you, if there was an emotional attachment, I was your people pleaser. This theme had been repeated throughout my life, putting others ahead of myself. It's still a struggle today, though I'm light-years better.

Let this story, and the accompanying three-plus years of harsh judgment, the six years of PTSD symptoms, be your warning.

Love yourself. Respect yourself. Be vulnerable with people you trust.

You deserve it, no matter how much you've convinced yourself otherwise.

You're not stupid; you're not weak; you're a human being. You're still learning. Take the lessons of your trauma and wield them with a sense of strength and pride in yourself.

CHAPTER THIRTEEN

LIVING IN DARKNESS

*"They wander in darkness seeking light,
failing to realize that the light is
in the heart of the darkness."*

—Manly P Hall
The Lost Keys of Freemasonry

THERE ARE TWO WAYS TO EXPLAIN what "darkness" is. One I will explain in great detail. The other, not so much, but it has been clear throughout the book thus far and will be touched on at the end.

First, follow me on this . . .

Let's assume your day job isn't carpentry of any kind.

You may not understand how to hammer two pieces of wood together (properly), but most people can figure out how to hammer a nail into something. First, you hold the nail upright. Grab a hammer. Tap the head of the nail a couple times to get it into the wood just enough so you can take your hand away and it'll stay upright. Next, you hammer it harder until the head of the nail is flush with the wood.

Not discussing brain surgery here.

Now imagine you have to do it in a dark and extremely loud room, and there's a timer of one minute.

You are scared you might hurt yourself while hammering because you can't see, the noise is distracting, and you have to get it done in a certain amount of time. Anxiety kicks in, your hands might shake, but hurry up because time is running out. Find the hammer, the nail, try to follow the same pattern. But don't waste time. How much has passed? What happens if you don't get it done in time? Am I going to smash myself with this hammer?

Anyone who automatically thinks this would be a breeze has never been under pressure and done basic firearm drills on a range at the same time. Just that little bit of extra pressure can completely throw you off if you can't keep your head straight and focused.

This is a pretty good example of what it is like to live in darkness.

The task itself is easy. The confusion, the distractions, the anxiousness, the feeling like you're running out of time, that will throw you off.

My dad died 10 years ago. I went through all the phases of grieving. I suffered deeply, as I needed to. It seemed like my entire world had come undone. My dad was my best friend, my confidant, my mentor, my teacher, idol, hero, all that. When he first told me he had cancer my sister was with me. She broke down crying. I just sat on the recliner unable to comprehend any of it.

He said, "I have stage 4 cancer. I'm sorry and I hope you can both forgive me for any wrong I have ever done."

What? Dad has cancer? What does "stage 4" mean? How long does he have? Is it treatable? It is curable? What the hell? I thought to myself.

My dad went into remission after months of chemotherapy but never quit smoking cigarettes. It was only eight months after he told he had cancer that he died.

I lived with him almost entirely during this time. I was there to help where I could and mostly just be company for him. Honestly, I did a shitty job. I was 16, I didn't really think about what was happening.

He would tell me I could lie in his bed with him when he went to sleep. I did a couple of times and we would talk but more often than not I was fucking around on the computer. I had a lot of shame for a long time over this as I felt that I should have spent more time with him when he needed me most.

I rarely saw my mom during this period, so I went to stay with her for a weekend. I set up my dad's place as much as I could before I left.

On the way out I said, "alright dad, I'll be back Monday. Love you." He just nodded.

"Dad, I love you." I looked back at him. We were never afraid or shy of telling each other we loved each other (although, as I entered my teens years hugs turned to handshakes and head nods, as is the natural progression for most men with dads like mine).

"Love you, too," he said quietly.

I didn't think much of it.

Monday rolled around and I went home. His nurse was trying to get into the apartment. I let her in. We weren't exactly the cleanest people but his place *trashed*. The nurse immediately went to him. It was like he was drunk. She told me she thought he'd mixed up his medications and needed to go to the hospice immediately.

I didn't know what a hospice was. I knew that was where his home care came from but I had no idea it was the final destination for so many people. I just rolled it off as okay; he needs to go get right.

I drove him there. I tried to talk to him on the way but it was like he couldn't make the words come out right. Not a lot of what he said made sense.

I went in and hung out with him in the room for a bit. I started to cry. I saw the massive pain he was in. I knew it was horribly bad. Seeing me crying he tried to reassure me it was all going to be okay. I didn't reply. I just wanted to see the doctor.

I didn't want to call anyone yet. The nurse I met at my dad's apartment called my mom and told her what was going on. She showed up at the hospice shortly after me. My sister followed soon after. I remember arguing with them that no one was going to call Michigan (where all of my dad's side of the family lives) until we heard from the doctor. Why cause that kind of stress if this is nothing?

The doctor came in. Within a minute he told me I needed to call Michigan.

My father was dying.

I left his room for a moment. I went into the hallway and wasn't sure how to process this news. It didn't take me long but I called my grandma. My Uncle Pat answered and I told him what was going on. He spread the word for me. Doesn't mean my phone didn't ring but he tried to minimize it as much as he could. I never thanked him for that. Wish I could.

Family flew down quickly. Seeing my grandma get upset over this was hard to watch. Seeing my aunts distraught was hard too. But witnessing his younger brother, the brother he owned the pizzeria with, his best friend, break down over this was one of the hardest things I've had to stomach. It broke my heart to see him in that state. At that time he was the uncle who clearly never dealt with children but was always fun to be around. Least, that's how I saw him. I never saw him cry or scream—like he did when he saw my dad.

During this time in the hospice I hung around my sister and her boyfriend, Collar, who was also a good friend of mine. I would sometimes talk to my dad. The hospice gave me a booklet that said the last sense to go is hearing. Could be something they tell the living to make us feel better, of course, but it made me feel like I could frame the right words.

Looking back, saying goodbye to him didn't make me feel any better about the situation. I would say something entirely different today than I did then. Saying what I said to him over the couple days he was in there didn't really give me any sense of closure.

He died a couple of days after he arrived at the hospice.

I drove home and felt numb. Just as I felt when I woke up to my grandma crying because she watched him take his final breathe. I was in the chair next to the bed and woke up, realizing what had just happened and thought to myself, *that's that. He's gone.*

What happened after he died is a blur. I only remember bits and pieces of his funeral. Part of what my sister said. Part of what I said. Part of what my uncles said. I only remember a few of the other mourners.

What I do remember afterwards was the influx of drugs I started to take. Anything to just not feel the avalanche of emotions. I was living in darkness but trying to illuminate my life with drugs.

The chapter *Drugs* painted a pretty good picture of how that works out . . .

Back then I went in reverse. I became much more aggressive. I rebelled in any way I could. My mom had no control over me. No one did. I made myself as alone as I felt I was.

I think this is a relatively easy-to-understand concept most people have experienced at some point in their lives. Someone you know dying is a miserably dark experience, especially if they were close to you.

When I was 14 years old I became a neo-Nazi.

I wish I could respect you, as the reader, and explain why but I can only remember so much of my mindset at that time. What I can remember is that I learned that America and the Axis Powers had a treaty (which the attack on Pearl Harbor broke). I didn't learn this in school. When I asked my teacher, he sort of mumbled, "yes, there was," and immediately got off the subject.

The website I learned this piece of information from was a sister-site of the largest neo-Nazi website out at that time. I never saw looking at information as scary. After all, I was told to stay away from Satanism and doing the exact opposite worked out well for me.

Fuck it, let's go down this rabbit hole and see what else I'm not being taught.

I classified myself as a neo-Nazi or "skinhead" from 14 until I denounced it at 21.

Interesting seeing that I attached to that kind of lifestyle as I was following a philosophical path created by LaVey, a Mexican American from Jewish decent. Even more interesting, a multitude of others in that lifestyle had the same philosophical views as I did. Like so many other ideas we held, it was a hypocrisy we were willing to ignore. Ultimately the two are entirely separate ideologies, LaVeyan Satanism being for yourself and Nazism being for the state and race.

None it made my life any better, least not till the very end, and even that was a sort of blessing in disguise.

I made a lot of friends in that world. My presence was recognized by the higher-ups as valuable. At one point I was up to be the Florida Representative but it ultimately never happened.

Being a neo-Nazi almost got me expelled from high school, twice. Once for national socialist artwork in my graphics class. Once for vandalism around school. I was in a *Sixty Minutes* documentary shaking hands with a leader of my organization giving the Seig Heil–Nazi–salute. A teacher once called me out for the documentary while I was in college. I wrote a paper on leadership, highlighting Adolf Hitler as an archetypally strong leader. I gave a presentation on that paper to a full class. I had a couple of neo-Nazi-related tattoos that I have had lasered and covered since. But it also gave me purpose. Truthfully, in some ways, being a neo-Nazi is often easier than not.

It gives you someone to blame.

When you're involved in any extremist group you can scapegoat your issues onto other people with ease. Most of the stuff I bitched about back then was trivial to my life but I made it my business anyway.

I would join marches. I went to the national meetings. I kept in regular contact with my friends from that world. When I was 19 I dated a neo-Nazi for about a year (who knew mutual hatred masking drastic insecurities was a love language?). Shortly before I left the organization, and neo-Nazism as a whole, I had planned to go with them on the Mexico-Arizona border and run patrols, similar to the Minute Men. Basically, the organization I was in would go on the border and track illegal immigrants trying to get into the country. They had an extremely effective system for doing this and almost always caught someone, or so I was told.

My actions were dictated by living by that creed. I would bully my peers at school because they were gay, or Hispanic, or black. I took every opportunity to let everyone know I wasn't afraid of the consequences of my beliefs. While it is arrogant for me to believe this intimidated people, maybe it did. Even when my perceived enemies approached me, I never backed down. I stood my ground every time. No one ever did a thing, no matter how many times I squared off, which at one point was a pretty regular thing. The more it happened, the more I pushed the envelope. What would've been two people bitching at each other turned into me looking at non-whites and throwing up the Nazi salute, at times directly in their face.

Anti-fa would come oppose us. We had a couple run ins with them at rallies or meetings. They were nowhere near as relevant then as they are today. You can partly thank them and the media for the rise in neo-Nazism in America. I don't think the organization I was in wasted funds on marketing. They didn't need to. Once they pulled the permit for the rally, word got out. The media would sensationalize the event, this attracts anti-fa to carry out their extremely fascist tactics, and before you know it there is a *Unite The Right* battle in the streets.

That's a harsh reality for you, dear reader. If you go to rallies to make noise to drown out whatever the neo-Nazis are saying, you are partly to blame, along with the media, for their rise. If a neo-Nazi organization comes to town, and someone has an interest in those beliefs, they can just as easily go to the rally, stay quiet, and research more when they get home. The people who are attracted to this lifestyle are going to admire the half-assed militant march the neo-Nazis do as opposed to the pink-haired 20-year-old screaming and jumping around.

The best recruitment the organization used was anti-fa and the media. They did the work for us.

That and the world wide web.

This idea of "Punch Nazis" is equally retarded. If the neo-Nazi is a skinhead following the old school rules, congratulations! You busting his lip means he spilled blood for his race. You just graduated him from white laces to red. If the neo-Nazi doesn't care about the old skinhead ways, still, congratulations! You just made them a hero among their brothers. As far as they see it, that neo-Nazi might have a busted eye or lip—might have even got their ass absolutely stomped—but they are also now a warrior of the white race, because of you. You just legitimized everything they believe in.

When dealing with this type of situation, it is important to remember the following words . . .

"If you know the enemy and know yourself, you need not fear the result of a hundred battles. If you know yourself but not the enemy, for every victory gained you will also suffer a defeat. If you know neither the enemy nor yourself, you will succumb in every battle."

-Sun Tzu, *The Art of War*

I understand these people infuriate you. I understand you hate them and everything they stand for. I understand why. I've seen it from that side and whether you like it or not, the truth is your loud opposition fueled my drive. I wouldn't say totally ignoring them is the answer but at the same time, the more you hyper focus on a problem, the easier it is for the solution to get lost in the noise.

The best advice I can give to break down the barrier with someone in that lifestyle is to *find commonality, exploit it, add humor. Repeat regularly.* Eventually the separatist won't want to separate themselves from people they see themselves in. People with whom they find commonality and humanity.

Anyway . . .

I think it must have given me this sort of false power that I craved. At 14 and throughout the years that followed I felt powerless and like nothing was within my control. Shitty stuff was happening to me and I felt I could blame everyone else. I felt like I saw the truth and everyone else was blind. Everyone was a sheep. I was one of the very few who was actually awake to such issues.

Getting involved in neo-Nazism is really no different than getting involved in a gang. The historical stuff might have been my introduction but the brotherhood you found was what kept me. I had Jewish friends, Hispanic friends, and black friends when I started to get involved. None of those relationships were like the relationships I found among my white brothers. It wasn't just "white brother" as in we are both white people. It was "white brother who is willing to fight for our race and tradition." The relationships with those people just felt different. It's difficult to explain unless you've felt any kind of "brothers in arms" feeling. It was what kept me involved.

There were two moments I can think of that lead to my departure. The first, a cross and swastika burning.

I was 19 and at a rally. The leader of the organization I was in was strongly against infighting within white nationalist groups. He saw it as far more important to join arms and unify a goal for an all-white homeland. Makes sense strategically. So at rallies we would host you could almost always find the Ku Klux Klan (KKK) in close trail behind us.

I fucking *loathed* the Klan. *"We 'ate coloruds because our daddies 'ated coloruds and our granddaddies 'ated coloruds and our great-granddaddies 'ated coloruds and that's juh what dah fuck we do. We 'ate coloruds."*

As far as I was concerned (then and now), that was their entire reasoning. It wasn't based on anything but blind hatred. There's obvious matching between what I believed and what they believe but still, I couldn't stand them. I despised seeing then at rallies. Most of those who stood next to me with swastika badges felt exactly the same way. There was this sort of childishness that was attached to those who marched and sang "white power," which was a Klan mantra. We said "Seig Heil," a phrase based in history and follows Nazism, a political structure, atop our pretentious thrones. The KKK was just hating for the sake of hating.

The after-rally party was hosted by the Klan. This meant a cross and swastika burning. I'm going to guess most of you have never bore witness to this type of thing so I'll paint the picture for you. Between the neo-Nazis and Klan there was about 50-70 of us. Men, women, and children were all there. There was a pig roast and plenty of booze to go around. The property was easily 10+ acres, surrounded by a high tree line, somewhere outside of Nashville, Tennessee. Sorry to disappoint, but if you photo edited the shirts people were wearing and removed the cross and swastikas, it would've looked like any large get-together on someone's property. People congregated in their groups and had what would look like totally normal conversations from the outside.

In an open part of the property there was Klansmen setting up two crosses and one swastika. I remember one of the Klansmen saying they didn't soak the cross and swastika in kerosene properly so they probably wouldn't burn as long as they hoped.

I was excited to see it. The elders in the organization spoke highly of the spectacle. But when my grandiose idea of feeling at one with my brothers as we watched a swastika light the sky met reality, I was disgustingly disappointed.

"We gadder unner da cross and swastiker wit our brudders in black..."

Here we go, mother fucker! Light that shit up! I thought to myself as the adrenalin started to pump.

"... We are da chitlen of God! Da chosen people of our Lord an' Savior Jesus Christ!..."

Christian Identity... What an idiot.

(If you don't know, Christian Identity is a religion some of these people follow that basically states Aryans are the true children of God and will return to Jerusalem. Coloreds are mud people, basically a creation of all things evil and impure. I wish this was a joke, and it is, but it also isn't.)

Clearly wasted out of his mind, a friend of the KKK kept interrupting from the side. A slur of drunken *"white power!"* and *"fuck niggers!"* came out of this fool for a solid five minutes before someone finally got him to shut up.

The Grand Wizard leading the ceremony never broke cadence. I'm sure overly drunk idiots were a regular occurrence for him at these ceremonies.

It didn't take long but soon the excitement I originally had dissipated. I looked around and saw the KKK in their hoods and saw them as the same antifa cowards who were just protesting us. They were sloppy. It was almost like they all had this aura of shit and you couldn't ignore it anymore.

I turned my attention back to the Grand Wizard with distain.

I sat there and listened to this toothless, mumbling, downright moron go on and on about how they light the cross to light the way of God in darkness. I put my head down and felt genuinely grossed out.

I have to call this dipshit my brother? This three-toothed fucking idiot? Is this what I want? The Klan? I thought to myself.

Well done. This guy, and the drunk idiot who won't stop interrupting him, are now alongside you in brotherhood. That cross burns next to the swastika, in case you didn't notice . . .

I kept to my neo-Nazi crowd all night, avoiding the KKK wherever I could. But I was no different from them, even if I thought I was at the time. My skinhead brothers and sisters snickered about them as we drank ourselves stupid.

I can say for sure this was the first time I was ever *truly* disgusted with this part of my life.

I was 20 years old and in Michigan working my pizzeria. One night I was dragged by my uncle and cousin to a club off Woodward Ave in downtown Detroit, very much in the ghetto. We were the only white people in the club. After the second rap-group brawl broke out I decided to wait for my family members outside. I tried to get them to go with me but they refused. Rap groups fighting in Detroit (at this time anyway) was a typical precursor to a club shooting.

Fuck this, I thought.

Outside of the club was a park bench where I waited for them. I was there maybe 10 minutes and this black woman sat down on the other side. I nodded in her direction but had no desire to talk.

She started talking to me but I gave little in return. She pressed me—charmingly—and we spoke for about a half hour. I found her to be incredibly friendly and even though I would never admit it at that time, uniquely attractive. I mentioned I was just getting ready to start college again as a history major.

"That's awesome! I'm a high school history teacher! So what's your favorite historical era?"

"I really like the Roman Empire and learning about the Axis Powers."

"Oh my God! I love World War II!"

"Right? I mean, who doesn't?"

Then it came. "Wait, you're not a neo-Nazi though, are you?"

I have no idea what made her ask. I didn't say or do anything that would give that information about myself away. Maybe she saw the tattoos on my arm? But it was pretty dark by that bench. I always shaved my head so maybe that's why. But so do many other people. I never saw that as enough of a reason for her to ask something like that. It remains a mystery in my life.

"Fuck no!" I replied—laughing.

Inside I was exploding with questions.

What the fuck did I just say? Did I just deny my beliefs? I never do that! I've squared off with 6 foot plus, 250 lbs., black men. I've marched with neo-Nazis. And pretty little 130 lbs., history teacher is who I deny my beliefs to?

Our conversation didn't last much longer as her friend exited the club and she left. I sat there in shock. Why, after years of being so proud of my beliefs, would I ever deny them? It doesn't matter that I'm off

Woodward Ave in Detroit. It doesn't matter that I'm the only white guy I see. You never deny yourself. You wear your colors on your skin and your allegiance is there in fresh black and red ink, in case you forget.

You don't deny that. Before that day, I never had.

I was in a sort of haze for the next couple of days. I couldn't get that conversation out of my head. I couldn't understand why it happened in the first place. Just like you're not supposed to deny your beliefs, you're also not supposed to engage the "enemy" if you don't have to and I didn't. I could've ignored her.

At that time, I wished I had.

Over the next year I had a pivotal mind-set shift. This sort of epiphany didn't happen quickly. I said what I said but I still felt the way I felt. I slowly started to notice a lot I didn't like in the organization. The members were majority hardcore drug addicts (I was using as well) but marching at rallies about how nonwhites are bringing drugs into the country.

We helped demand their supply.

Everyone in the organization was involved in some kind of drama with each other. I found myself turned off to it all. I started wondering what I was seeing in this mind-set.

I started to realize all of the benefits of knowing people from different backgrounds and cultures. I started to notice the vast similarities between Communism and National Socialism (Nazism), and to this day, as far as I'm concerned, both are fast highways to the complete destruction of a society.

For a while I thought Fascism without the usage of eugenics was a better path to focus on but that didn't last long.

I started to wonder about everything I had missed out on because of my beliefs. *Who* did I miss out on because of my beliefs?

I eventually decided I didn't want that lifestyle anymore. I decided to leave it behind. I renounced the brutal beliefs I had held onto for far too long.

And I'm ten times the man because of it.

Seven years of living in that darkness. It doesn't mean there weren't inspiring, amazing, eventful, even beautiful moments of light during that time. Of course there were. But it was exceedingly rare that those moments happened solely because I was a skinhead. Some of the best bonding times I had with those I had formed closed relationships with had absolutely nothing to do with us being involved in the life. Our friendships were like any other. We would go to concerts together, drink together, party together. Only thing that really made our non-lifestyle activities any different was the brands we put on ourselves.

For a couple months when I was 19 I had two other skinheads living with me. They went out to a bar one night and came back to see me playing video games on a couch. They made me pause my game. I guess when they were out at the bar they got to talking about me and decided they needed to push me to return to college. They declared my mind was too good to waste and a better education would enable my opportunities to skyrocket.

In the chapter *Drugs* I credit my interest in military intelligence as the catalyst for my goals heading in that direction. One of the skinheads was a former military policeman (the other was the first person I ever felt the need to pull a gun on, but that's a different story). He was the first person I ever heard explain what contracting companies do after I foolishly confessed trying to find loopholes so I could join the military.

I'm where I am today, in my career, because a neo-Nazi roommate encouraged me to go back to college and get my degree. I lived in darkness for seven years only to have it encourage me to move in the right direction.

My life as a skinhead got me interested in history in the first place. My life as a skinhead introduced me to a man who urged me to study it further. And I did. And it was in college I met a friend who had switched to an entertainment industry school. I spoke with him about his experience there and decided I would go there for grad school. It was in grad school I started my music company.

Did I need seven years of my life consumed by that neo-Nazi darkness to get me on the right track? I wish I could say otherwise but at the same time, perhaps curiously, I don't. It worked out the way it did and while I no longer hold those beliefs I don't necessarily regret those days. They played a part in my current position in life.

If I were a man who believed in fate, I would see this period as something I had to endure, following the true stoic path. As previously mentioned in the chapter *Foundation*, I don't believe in fate. All the same, seeing that side of life, that side of humanity, changes your perspective on humanity. I wouldn't say it was for better or worse (for every skinhead at a rally there was twenty opposing us), just something I see today as interesting. Dark, horrible, ugly, but interesting.

Upon all of this, knowing that I choose to leave, something that some of my closest friends were adamantly against, is a thing of pride. This is just one example of this but I *chose* to be a better man, at a time, and in many circumstances, where I didn't *need* to be.

My mind-set as a neo-Nazi was arguably the opposite of Luciferianism in every way (remember, I didn't have these philosophical views at that time—though my interest in paganism was sparked out of this lifestyle). As I've made very clear by now, Luciferians hold personal accountability in a high regard. As do the Satanists. Thelemites. Stoics. Objectivists. Neo-Nazis blame everyone else for their perceived or real shortcomings. When I was involved in that world I didn't see it like that and I doubt most neo-Nazis, skinheads, white nationalists, white separatists, whatever you want to call them, see it like that either.

To continue, science plays a pretty significant role in why I follow philosophical paths that I do (Hermeticism, anyone?). A lot of the "science" you learn as a neo-Nazi is complete and utter bullshit. One of the main eugenics studies they reference is based on the findings of an author with ties to the KKK. Wonder if he was biased? I was never a Holocaust denier, though many who stood next to me were, but there is "science" to back up those ideas well. Re-educating yourself is an important part of anyone getting out of that life, and honestly, it's hard. Not just to relearn what you got wrong, but to dismiss some of the information you learned that was actually factual (stuff like crime statistics, ghetto population numbers, etc.). Understanding that there are circumstances outside of race that contribute to these statistics took me a while to fully grasp.

That lifestyle is lived according to the 14 words—*We must secure the existence of our people and a future for white children*—said by David Lane. But as someone who was not born into that mind-set, lived with those beliefs for years, and has now left, I can confidently say it is all about failing to understand your own shortcomings and a desire for power. I think every detailed belief within neo-Nazism can come back to those two points.

My father's death imprisoned me in an immense and cold darkness but my rebellion was the light. And what an important and useful light it has proved to be! This dark time was imperative to helping me discover my real self as a young man. Without his death, and furthermore, consistent influence in my life, I might still be trying to be the man *he* wanted me to be, versus the man *I* had to be.

Living in darkness is difficult. Every Luciferian knows this. But if there is anything we collectively agree on it is that in darkness we grow and evolve as human beings. It is in darkness that we get just a little closer to reaching our individual apotheosis. I can confidently say that so far in my life every major point of darkness has led me to a glorious moment of light.

The second way to interpret darkness is more in an occult sense. By occult I mean "hidden knowledge." So studying the occult is another way to visit darkness.

I came to Luciferianism from Satanism. I came to Satanism from Catholicism. Catholics are famous for pushing a fire-and-brimstone narrative, so in that sense I was willing to look at darkness, a sort of fear, and try to understand it further. The absolute last thing Catholics want you to do is study Satanism of any kind. Of course this made it all the more alluring to me.

Growing up I was told to stay away from the methods of Satan and Lucifer (my parents used their names interchangeably, not because they understood the difference. Catholics . . .). As an adult I embrace it and the tables have turned. Now I see Catholicism (a religion built on submission to the church) as a darkness just as they would see my philosophical views in that way.

It's not always a tough time in life. To say I was living in darkness when my father died is accurate. Same applies for my skinhead days. To say I was exploring darkness when I found Satanism is also accurate. Same theme, but two totally different situations and outcomes.

To conclude, "darkness" is not a different word for "evil." In the example I used at the start of this chapter, where do you see evil? Noise is not evil. A dark room is not evil. Timers aren't evil. Neither is the hammer and nail. These are just the circumstances and tools, but individually they are not "evil."

Darkness is ignorance. It is the absence of truth. It's working your way through the maze, regardless of what that "maze" actually is.

CHAPTER FOURTEEN

FREEDOM AND MORALITY

"Do what thou wilt shall be the whole of the Law."

—Aleister Crowley
The Book of the Law

IF FREEDOM MEANS ACTION, then morality is its police.

No freedom has served me more than my escape from religious dogma as set forth by Catholicism. Cutting that cord revealed more to me about the world we live in, the laws we follow and the paths we walk than anything else ever has. It has allowed me to question everything I was told to believe and filter out what didn't make sense. Plenty was filtered out. A lot was left behind and forgotten. Many of those values were rebelled against. All the same, many of those values still held true.

How many of those values were exclusively Catholic? If I had to explain the pagan ethos I would say it is the mentality of "honor your gods." If I had to do the same for Gnosticism I would say it is—ideally—the mentality of "live like Christ." Luciferian ethos would be "become a Light Bearer." While these might seem superficially to be different ethical codes to live by it doesn't mean they are never interchangeable. For example, Jesus said to honor your father and mother. Roman pagans didn't have the same set of rules that Christianity did but the idea is still the same. This can be proven by looking at how they presented themselves. If a Roman male was asked his name, it would often include his own, plus that of his fathers and family surname. The same goes for the Celts. One implication is that they held the same beliefs as Christians about honoring their family. To dishonor the family was both a disgrace in pagan religions and in Abrahamic ones.

Seeing as I left religious dogma behind as a young child I had to explore the majority of my life questioning what was acceptable and what was not. LaVeyan Satanism initially gave me a great guide to figure most of it out but I still had to make the ultimate decision myself. I was forced to study and inquire about the world around me on my own terms. Of course I was influenced but the definitive results were mine to choose.

As the chains fell, I felt their weight drop away. As the walls around me collapsed, I was blinded by the sublime incoming light. As I listened, I heard the snake hiss to me. The secret was revealed and like Eve, I had eaten from the Tree of Knowledge. I had begun to climb the ladder to my apotheosis. The serpent's voice still rings through me today. I can still hear his divine hiss. I know that I will not die from dipping into this pool of reality. But the freedom still came with the burden of choice. I was now responsible to lead a life in line with my new sense of morality, which I consistently questioned, and come up with the answers to life's questions on my own.

I had no idea what my life would now entail. I had no clue about the amount of work that would be required of me. I was being forced to see the world around me without the airbrushing and special effects. Admittedly it looked ugly at first. I saw the bad before I saw the good. I had to. Just as no good exists without the bad, no light exists without the darkness, and both must be witnessed and experienced to the core for the Luciferian to appreciate them. Still, it was the darkness I saw first.

Out of that primeval gloom I formed my worldview. Before I recognized the light Lucifer provides me, my mind-set was tainted by ideas formulated through hatred. That hatred grew the profound blackness that had surrounded me just for a moment into an all-enveloping stench that would ultimately surround me for nearly a decade. During this time I was trying to live freely but unable to see that I had cast my own chains, and those chains themselves had weights that were bolted to the ground. The knowledge I was attempting to gain was inhibited by my prejudice against outsiders.

Fortunately, I started to grow beyond it. I no longer saw myself in that world. I was happy about its outcome and it also was a catalyst that skyrocketed me into further education. I combined that schooling with a new goal, the first I had formulated and realistically attempted to achieve. I was now living entirely free from my caged mind-set for the first time. My actions existed because I wanted them to exist, not because I thought they should. Suddenly they were natural and achievable. I was driven to succeed, utilizing the lessons I'd learned from the darkest times—and for the first time able to envisage my future path.

All of this brought me to the place I'm in right now. There are devils and angels all around me. Some of them I created. Some of them found me. All the same, my decisions, my actions and the space I occupy are my responsibility. My space is constantly growing, constantly evolving. It has been built, torn down, rebuilt, sculpted, disengaged, engaged and given life. None of this would have been possible without the freedom that I chose to acknowledge when I was a child.

With all of the freedom I have given myself, why do I chose this place? Why did I come back a third time to re-edit this book? Why did I make the decisions I made? Why did I find this philosophical path as opposed to others?

The answer is simple. It's because it is what I have chosen. And I am free to do whatever else I choose.

You might think LaVey, but the truth is Crowley is where I developed most of my ideas relating to freedom.

Whether it is believed or not, all major Left Hand Path philosophy leaders believe in some kind of morality. From Crowley to LaVey—even Greaves—agree that some kind of morality is expected of the individual. For instance, the quote at the start of the chapter, "Do as thou wilt shall be the whole of the Law," Crowley is still acknowledging there is, in fact, a law that accompanies life, which he termed Thelema. LaVey had his Nine Satanic Sins and Greaves has his Seven Fundamental Tenets. All these men embrace the idea of freedom and they all understood that a basic form of morality keeps them in line with their personalized, long-term ethos.

Freedom is a beautiful gift to give yourself until morality demands its dues—and it will. Just like you can't receive a gift of over $10,000 without paying taxes on it, you can only enjoy so much freedom until morality checks you. I think it plays into the balance we all try to observe, but in the moment that I am testing the limits of my morality, I want to tip those scales as much as I can in thought or action.

Morality is fluid. The religious right wants you to believe that morality is as concrete as the Lincoln Memorial but back here in reality we know that isn't true. I am skeptical of any adult who continues to hold the same values they did as a young child. What a child thinks is acceptable and what an adult should think is acceptable may have some trifling similarities, but overall a child's worldview is not solidified simply because they cannot fully understand the world they have not yet experienced. As far as I am concerned, this restricts the freedoms of *both* the immature and the fully developed individual.

But that's kind of the point . . .

If the child grows up in fear of embracing full freedom they will still never dare taste it as an adult. How sad that when he or she's old, they've never been free. They have never tried drugs fearing they would get addicted, or even more pathetically caught. They never missed a Sunday Mass. They never ate a meal without giving thanks. They never partied much but especially not during a working week. They never abandoned themselves to carnal pleasures before marriage and not much even afterward. After all, sodomy is a sin.

They always did their homework. They always came home on time. Curfew was parental law and better not break that. Can't *possibly* disregard your parents. They never gulped a bottle of their favorite liquor. They always showed up to work on time. They never called in sick because they were never so hungover they couldn't get out of bed.

They never drove in the country back roads in a lifted truck after too many brews at the local watering hole. They never did a line of white in the bathroom at a house party. They never fucked that cute redhead who's all over them. They never fought their friends with bare fist and hugged afterward with busted lips and black eyes. They never told a cop to fuck off. They never had to convince the bartender they weren't ready to be cut off. They never stayed awake for three days straight strung out on acid and ecstasy. They never set a couch on fire just to watch it burn.

So far, so adolescent. But the daring goes much, much deeper . . . They never studied Plato and Nietzsche. They never listened to Hawking. How dare he try to replace religion with horrible, ungodly science! They never questioned their lifestyles. They never even thought to question God—and furthermore is their God the right God?

It might suit their lifestyle but without the willingness to risk everything they'll never know if a better lifestyle—or a better God—exists.

Nope. They were righteous—and self-righteous—their entire life.

They dismissed everything that looked dangerous, whether or not it actually was. They took no risks. They never challenged their thought process. A bulbous ego was attached to their belief system but they became so painfully brainwashed into thinking their way of life was automatically the best way of life, they never sought for more. Or not even necessarily more, but what else? Their belief system imprisoned them in fear but their egos were too strong to realize it.

If they were scared of our scientific leaders because they saw their findings as a challenge to God, is that not a rejection of God's awesome power and creation, in their worldview? If God is responsible for the heavens and earth—as noted in Genesis—isn't science going to be a part of that creation as well?

Without testing their morals they have never seen what its limits could—even should—be. Their morality is therefore weak. *The hypothesis has not been tested.* It's just an idea. Others can test it as much as they want but the only outcome that can be seen by Mr. and Ms. Do-Good is when freedoms are taken too far. And even for a Left Hand Path practitioner, there is a distinct limit. We soon learn the hollowness of doing what "we wilt" without living under our true will, or law. We are brutally honest with ourselves and equally expect others to take their own responsibility for their excesses . . .

As far as they are concerned, the idea of a functioning addict is bullshit; they are still addicts. The idea of someone testing the limits of the law is null and void; they are still criminals. The thought that you can enjoy someone's body without enjoying their company is absurd; you're just a tramp.

All or nothing. Black and white. This or that. This is really how some people live and think. The fact remains that staying "safe" isn't the answer. It never can be.

Well Mr. and Ms. Do-Good, I am sorry to inform you that your entire life has never been lived. You have never sought out that adrenaline surge. You never took as much as you could from life. You never tasted freedom. You are like an animal that was born in captivity. You think you have it good because you are fed and taken care of. But you never enjoyed the thrill of the hunt. You never tested a single limit because the very idea of doing so frightened—and ultimately paralyzed you.

It's not your fault. You were lied to. You were misdirected.

The weak-willed cannot handle freedom. I get it and honestly I don't mean that as an insult. I understand the benefits and security you get with a safety net. A steadfast life is one I am not against by any means. I've usually found that order and will wins every time over chaos created by embracing freedom. The difference is I understand what lies beyond the freedoms I allow myself. I know what happens when I take my morality and break it because I've already taken care to field-test it. Before it became a rule I live by I understood what it was like to live beyond it.

Nikki Sixx of Motley Crue famously said, "Once you taste excess, everything else tastes bland." How true. The excess is nothing other than the freedom you permit yourself. It can always be taken too far. And once that point is reached, as Nikki Sixx said, "everything else tastes bland." This can result in a too obsessive quest for new freedom after new freedom which, in turn, can be dangerous. The desire for higher risk becomes almost too profound and starts to enter dangerous territory.

Not every moral needs to be tested. I don't need to harm an innocent person to understand its pointlessness. I never had the urge to test certain values because on a basic human level I understand why they exist. Christians like to argue that without Christianity communities we would still be sacrificing humans to pagan gods. In part they are right. The Spanish conquerors, for example, put an end to the Mayans' age-old sacrificial rituals. But we can't judge any society today on values it held centuries ago (life and common values even 100 years ago were radically different from today). They aren't even remotely the same. I think at some point we would have understood, collectively, as a society, we just didn't need to do it any more.

So if you are wondering if I have ever practiced or felt the need to practice ancient pagan rituals, like bloodletting or sacrifice, the answer is a definitive no. A bleed-through effect of the Satanic Panic of the 1980s would have you believe otherwise but that is far from the truth. The Satanic Panic was based, in part, on an extremely small group of individuals acting out against all religions and the Christian church. But it was nothing more than a witch hunt completely unfounded in actual threats.

Freedom can go seriously wrong. When it meets lack of empathy it can become dangerous. The freedoms I allow myself are influenced by a variety of outside factors, some legal, some ethical. Though when legal ramifications or ethical practice do not influence the individual we will often see them commit crimes we would consider heinous.

When this type of person feels that they need to sacrifice a life source to Lucifer they will murder the victim in cold blood. To them this is acceptable because they believe their religion told them it was. It is no different than the church validating murder during the Crusades. Although killing another human is not necessary to give thanks to Lucifer and murder is against Christianity it does not and did not stop these people from embracing the freedoms they allowed themselves. The Crusaders still killed in the name of Christ, as did the Spanish Inquisition.

Therefore freedom has the potential to be ruinously dangerous—and must be explored with caution. Regardless of what deity you follow.

I was maybe 18 or 19 and spent a weekend at an old friend's house. This weekend was going to be filled like any other we spent together, boozing, loud music and girls. In no time we had invited over two women and another male friend of ours. Shortly after they arrived the drinking started and the deck of cards was out. In a matter of 30 minutes the men were down to our boxers and the women were nude. Within the hour I experienced my first orgy.

One of the guys and one of the girls had a thing for each other and decided to consolidate their relationship at the end of the weekend. The girl was riding with me back to Fort Lauderdale because she was meeting a friend of hers over there a couple days later. I had known her for a while. We were occasional friends with benefits.

It's the second day at my place and I was watching a hockey game. She stayed in my guest room and went to bed before the game was over. Over the past weekend I made some kind of bet with her that if the Detroit Red Wings won she would have to let me fuck her butt. She was pretty confident they weren't going to win and agreed.

The Red Wings proved to be great wingmen and won the game. She texted me shortly after she went to bed.

"Who won?"

"Red Wings, duh."

"Oh shit. Oh well. Hey, didn't we have a bet?"

"Ya we did."

"Oh . . . Guess it's my time to keep my word. ;-)"

I had never fucked her in the ass before. I was stoked at the idea over the weekend and now she is here, in my guest room, ready for the fuckening. But she is now with my friend and I know they aren't in an open relationship.

"Ya it definitely would be . . . but you and (friend) are together now and I can't do that to him."

"Oh . . . okay. Goodnight."

"Night."

I had no reason to not fuck her besides loyalty to my friend. Though I laugh about the story now, it's something that men can relate to. An attractive woman is ready to be sodomized in your house but she is with your friend. What do you do? I'm not ashamed to admit it was hard to send her that reply. But I did, and that's what matters, not the temptation. Girl had a PhD in Nymphomania. You'd be tempted too.

Women like her have come and gone many times. It was not the first time a friend's girlfriend made a pass at me nor was it the last. It doesn't matter that the friend she was with and I don't talk today. It doesn't matter that she broke up with him three days later. It matters that in the moment I understood loyalty came before the desire. Part of my morality is to honor my relationship with my friends. That supersedes a desire to get laid any day of the week. I have never seen a woman so gorgeous that she is worth seriously damaging a friendship or violating my integrity.

I don't deserve a pat on the back. I didn't go above and beyond the call of duty here. I am a man and acted like one in the face of temptation. My morality stopped me from doing something that was against my values. It's that simple. I had the freedom to escalate what was in front of me but that would've meant betraying someone I was close to. Those ends never justify the means.

Though even this moral was formed because I knew what it was like to live on the other side of it. Long ago I knew someone who was admittedly clueless on all things women. Great person, incredibly kind, fun to hang out with, but next to zero education on how women think. We were close, and he was there for me when I needed him.

He had a crush. She wasn't into it. I got between them. This scummy move motivated this moral. I was better than that and so was he. Sometimes the best thing you can do is let go and hope they have better people in their lives now. People who deserve the value they bring to the table. At the time, I didn't.

I still cringe at this memory.

Having said that, I don't see myself as morally superior to the next person. I'm sure a myriad of people would take exception to certain of my morals. And that's okay. I don't hold these values for them. I'll even admit that the morals I do possess are probably significantly fewer than the average person's.

There are really only so many things that I adamantly disagree with and even then there are certain extreme circumstances when I could choose to break or not follow these rules I live by. Unlike the mind-set of Mr. and Mrs. Do-Good, I think nearly everything falls into a shade of gray.

My morality is not a convenience. I often see people who will tell someone they hold certain values but actually do the opposite. I try my absolute hardest to not be one of them. Which is why I only hold a few absolute truths, where only extreme circumstances would allow them to be broken.

I have plenty good ideas. Nice, safe, fun-to-live-by ideas but only a couple of morals. An example of an idea I like is to treat your fellow man with respect. But this isn't a moral because I can think of far too many situations where my fellow man doesn't deserve to be respected. An example of a true moral is to never betray a friend's trust, whether in confidence or with something they did. It was their decision, not mine and therefore it is not my place to make their secrets public—or far worse, use it against them.

So far having this mind-set has worked pretty well in my favor, illuminating my actions and upholding my integrity.

The freedoms I explored led me to the values I now hold dear. Seeing as morality is fluid I accept that as I grow older and experience more that life has to offer, these morals might change. Perhaps even drastically. Though that change doesn't happen from restriction. No one ever grew living in a cage.

Certain animals can only grow physically to the size of their environment—only as much as their cage allows. The same goes with humans. Our physical capabilities are finite. But talk to someone who has tasted life and talk to someone who has overdosed on it. The person who has tasted life has an understanding of their potential. The person who overdosed on life understands that their ambitions are as endless as the experiences any one individual can accumulate—which led them to the freedoms they allow themselves to explore. Their sanity, their worldview, their faith (or lack of) and their values are the morality that keeps them grounded.

CHAPTER FIFTEEN

LIFE IN LIGHT

> *"You could leave life right now.*
> *Let that determine what you do*
> *and say and think."*
>
> —Marcus Aurelius
> *Meditations*

STEP ONE TO UNDERSTANDING what it is like to live in "light" is to understand what "light" means in the first place.

I know at times I have expressed the concept of light like it is some kind of reward or trophy. It is. But it's a perspective change, not a gift.

Living in light means you are living in a certain state of mind. Just as living in darkness can negate your actual actions if your mindset is skewed, living in light is less about the circumstance and more about how you perceive it. It is also the consequence of your actions, just as living in darkness *can be* a consequence of your action. The cause or the effect.

Living in light brings a sense of profound confidence. You know undoubtedly that you are a Light Bearer and because of that your life is not only illuminated but it is also illuminating those around you—often the best feeling in the world. When we finish something for ourselves it feels great but when that same action also benefits those around us, those we care for in some way, it feels even better. We can now see our own true abilities in all their glory.

Living in light shows the importance of humor. Laughter is contagious and when we are laughing it is likely that those around us are joining in. A sense of humor is important for the Luciferian as it reminds us that not everything needs to be taken so seriously (personally, I approach philosophy with a sense of humor and skepticism as I find it helps me understand it in a lighter, less serious way which in turn keeps my standard that these are ideas and nothing else). Shit, even the things that actually *are* serious always have a funny side, even if the humor is dark or hard to find. We recognize this truth best when we are living in light.

Living in light makes everything seem, appropriately enough, lighter. The weight of our world still rests on our shoulders but it is no longer weighing us down. We lift it up with pride and a sense of accomplishment realizing that all along it was possible for us to conquer all aspects of our lives. The issues now seem small. The resolutions may take hard work but the outcomes, more often than not, are well worth it. We stop sweating the small stuff. We relax. We trust ourselves and the order of the world.

When we know that we possess the power within ourselves to tackle anything that comes our way, it uplifts us from the misery of doubt. We see ourselves as truly capable human beings with endless power to accomplish and excel our lives. The lies we tell ourselves fade back into the dark where they belong and the truth reveals itself to us. We live our lives with a sense of poetry in mind and purpose in action.

Self-hate becomes nonexistent. Self-love, in thought and action, is the only feeling left when we turn to look at ourselves. The reflection in the mirror is the person who is totally in love with themselves. We know improvement is always possible, always sought after, always desired but at the moment we simply feel happy with our current situation. It was earned. It was worked for. We respected and honored it and in turn, that self-respect and self-honor become overall life goals.

Determination runs rampant through us. We are driven, prepared, ready to set out and ride out our lives. We see the path we need to take. We understand it. We have prepared for the obstacles and laugh at the idea that they once seemed so hard to surpass. No hill is too tall. Nothing is too difficult to overcome.

We see the beauty in all things. What once looked ugly and useless now seems gorgeous and important. We also appreciate the moment that it looked ugly, realizing that for us to see it in this light we had to see it cloaked in that initial primeval darkness. We see the beauty in the darkness, realizing that it brought us to this exact moment of light and without it we would not have grown as we have.

The concept of "living in light" or "living in darkness" is going to sound like light-worker, hippie nonsense to some and I understand why. I would still argue that they are beneficial and easily comprehendible terms that all of those involved in the Left Hand Path will clearly understand. It is a reference to the Hermetic Principle of Polarity—"Everything is Dual; everything has poles; everything has its pair of opposites."

If we agree that "darkness" is another term for ignorance, or working through a personal maze, as discussed in *Living In Darkness*, wouldn't "life in light" just be the other end of that? The beneficial consequence of exploring your personal period of darkness? The other way to take this is that the closer you are to the Divine, the more "in light" you are. Opposing, the further you are from the Divine, the more "in darkness" you are.

Living in light can last a second, a day, a week, as long as you want. So long as you can maintain that open and eager mind-set and brush off the negativity that will undoubtedly try to butt its ugly head into your life you can maintain your light. It can be difficult to see the rays of sunshine in all the enveloping gloom. Just as a bright light will blind you if you have been in a dark room for too long, Lucifer's light can confuse us if we have forgotten how to properly recognize it.

The gods are never not with us. Inbedded into our soul, our Divine Spark, they reside within us. The bright path is always lit up but it will be impossible to see if we are only looking for darkness. When we are living in a perpetual fog it seems that all things are shadows. The Luciferian recognizes that life has a constant yin and yang—opposite-and-equal balance—in all aspects.

The balance of light and dark is a fundamental truth that must be acknowledged by the Luciferian and even more so appreciated and approached with a sense of respect.

If you get a new job that means that someone else did not. The light is your new job. The dark is the other individual is still searching for work. While the success of others is not our responsibility it does not mean that we should not recognize these negative impacts, if for no other reason than to fully appreciate our new opportunity!

On July 31, 2013 Rockstar Energy Mayhem Festival (Mayhem Fest) hit Tampa, Florida, during their 26-show tour. Unbeknown to them—and to me—this festival would send an unprecedented shockwave of light throughout my life. For the first time I would begin a job with real passion and not just for a quick buck. I believe it was my daemon who whispered the critical words of encouragement into my ear that galvanized me into such action.

Mayhem Fest has since been canceled but it was the next runner-up to Ozzfest. It was the heavy metal and hard rock version of Vans Warped Tour. A collection of 20-something bands of assorted notoriety on a touring festival. The headliners this year included Rob Zombie, Five Finger Death Punch, Amon Amarth, Machine Head and more. One band I wasn't really familiar with in particular caught my attention between the ones I wanted to see. This band was called Motionless In White.

I was roaming around the fairgrounds waiting for the next show I was interested in and I heard this creative, metalcore band performing. As I got closer I admired their stage presence and decided to stay and watch their show. Shortly after they started their song "America" I heard a voice in my head, one that was not my own, one that I was comfortable with, and it spoke four words that lead me into a light I had never considered before.

You can do this.

That's it. It said nothing more. I actually remember I turned around to see if someone was talking to me. No one was close enough. I turned back to the band and noticed something I never had really noticed before: the crew.

Security, stage hands, sound technicians, lighting directors, vendors, roadies, tour managers, press, publicists, office managers, cleaning crews, photographers, videographers, promoters, street team members, and of course, the musicians themselves. I had seen hundreds of bands by then but I had never noticed all the other people that came in their wake. Motionless In White put on a great performance that day but my attention was divided between them and all the others helping them perform. Why hadn't I noticed them before? Why was I noticing them now?

I spent the rest of the festival on the lookout for these assisting hands. I would watch them, not really sure of what exactly they were doing, with great fascination. My interest was growing fast and once back home I got down to some serious research.

I never once considered working in the music business prior to this festival. I was a drummer for 13 years but did not take it all that seriously, nor did I have the raw, natural talent. When my family moved from Michigan to Florida my mom and dad opened a nightclub. This nightclub hosted a variety of up-and-coming DJs and eventually it had a rock night. It was during these local shows that I fell in love with heavy metal. It was amazing for me to watch these guys perform, see a mosh pit and all of the fans headbanging. I was instantly hooked and immediately dropped any interest in the Top 40 artists I was regularly subjected to. This was where the real music was hiding.

Over the years my company, Protage, Inc, morphed quite a bit. Originally I wanted to work in tour management and touring security. The security end of this world involved too large of a start-up cost than I could cover, so I decided to start smaller. Tour managers do exactly what their jobs say; they manage bands while they tour, handling the logistics of the road. I fell into concert promoting during grad school and it ended up being nearly the entire direction my company took.

(This third edit is written during 2024, but for my own purposes, I have edited it as if it were 2021. I worked in the music industry for eight years before life pulled me in a completely different direction. A topic for another book, should there ever be one. As for this story, I was all in the music business at that time working as a concert promoter and artist manager.)

That day, during Motionless In White's set, I believe my daemon spoke to me. He opened my eyes to something that was always right in front of me. The gods do not create paths for us but rather shed light on the paths that we hadn't noticed before. At that time I was pretty clueless what I was going to do after college. President Obama's DOD budget cuts were already biting so I was floating back and forth between what kind of job in politics I could gain. My options were slim and I seemed to hit a wall everywhere.

Imagine in our current political climate the shitstorm that a former neo-Nazi would face if he ran holding any kind of right-wing views (which I have). I recognized it then. I would never hold a public position with my past. And that was in 2013, years before President Trump came along and everyone on the right was considered a Nazi.

It was finally clear. It clicked together like a buckle. I enjoyed working as an investor. Always have.

I've always loved music. I have a deep and very personal connection to certain bands and songs that resonate with me on an intimate level. I still listen to some of the same music I listened to when I was 11 years old. Top 40 musicians come and go all the time but the solid rock musicians of the 70s, 80s, 90s, 00s, 10s, 20s, they've stuck around.

It was only common sense to merge my interests in business and music. Granted, I am a couple of years late. I would kill to be able to tell my 18-year-old self to get into the music industry back then. But oh well. I didn't and there's no use moaning. The beautiful truth here is that this is something that comes naturally and happily. And it all started with four words I heard in the back of my head.

You can do this.

I see it as my daemon spoke the words. Of course, I could have just had a thought. Or be crazy. Either is totally possible. Though internally I don't think it was. I feel like it was something outside of me.

I was 14 years old when I got a call from a good friend of mine name Oli.

"Hey man. What do you think about volunteering as an actor for a 'haunted house'?"

"That sounds cool!"

I got the details and ran it by my mom. She wasn't crazy about the idea. She didn't like the thought of people exploiting her newly amputee son for the entertainment of others. Weird, I know. But I hassled her till she said yes. I was allowed to go. Oli picked me up and we went to a local amusement park where it was being held. I had often been there before but it was the first time I ever went in the back of the building. There had to be about 40–60 people there. I recognized a few, some of whom I hadn't seen in years. Some hadn't seen me since I had my legs amputated.

I was nervous. It had been just over two years since I was released from the hospital and I was still struggling to cope. I was able to maneuver my wheelchair pretty well by this time. I was able to transfer to the ground, a car or my bed, all with no issue. My only real problem was I still couldn't get past the staring and people seeing the scars on my legs and from the skin grafts. All that merciless staring bothered me. I didn't know what my role would be at this haunted house but I knew that I was absolutely going to be stared at. I anxiously wondered if I was going to be expected to expose my scars.

The person running the attraction became a close friend, who would be with my sister and me when my dad was in hospice. We'll call him Collar because he should've worn one to stop him running wild. When he saw me I think he got an erection because as I discovered, for the make-up artist he was, working with amputees is gold in the horror world. It's like the best subject they can have for a victim role, at least that's what he implied. He was very excited to work with me and I was caught off guard. I felt pretty uneasy about it all at first.

Collar sat down and we spoke for a bit about what I was comfortable doing and what was possible to do in our time frame. I told him I was pretty much cool with whatever he wanted to do. He was so excited that it became contagious. Still, I was extremely nervous. I tried to hide it.

At this point no one had really looked at me and explained that my amputations could have benefits. I still saw an amputee's life as a burden. I didn't understand how this could possibly benefit anyone.

Cue Collar, who was really excited about working with someone with no legs.

My first job in the haunted house was basically to crawl around and scream about my legs being cut off. I don't think I have ever experienced anything so nerve-wrecking in my entire life. I nearly vomited. We were tipped off when a group walking through the haunted house was about 15 seconds away. The first warning I got scared me pale. I was terrified. I was racing into a darkness that weighed on me unlike anything I'd ever experienced. I went from despising the staring to begging for it within a matter of an hour.

The first group that came through didn't really notice me much. I thought, *Phew, that was easy*. But then one of the helpers gave me some tips to get their attention.

Thanks, asshole. Alright, next group, let's get this over with, I thought.

Next group definitely noticed me. I heard a couple of them talking, confused about whether I didn't have legs. I was totally shocked. I didn't know that it wasn't really obvious. After all, where there should be knees and ankles and feet there are none.

But alas, some people like to question everything. Bless them.

The next group had a couple of people who decided to hang out for a bit and it was only when I started to crawl toward them that they ran off. The helper comes back up and says that was genius and to do it again. Truthfully it wasn't on purpose, I was just running out of room to crawl around. The following group came and looked. I crawled a little faster toward them and they all ran off.

Even now writing this I can't help but to smile and remember how good that felt. I had found a niche—something where my amputations could be beneficial. Finally. Only took two years but this was the greatest feeling ever. Goodbye burden. Hello advantage.

The next day I showed up earlier. Collar was finally able to get his rocks off and bloody up my legs. They looked gross. It was so cool. I couldn't crawl around on the floor with the make-up on my legs because it would be rubbed off so I was now in the so-called "Devil's Play Room." Oli was in there with a couple of other guys I knew and some I had just met. I discovered I went to the same school as most of these guys.

This was the most talked-about room in the haunted house. It got the best reactions. We staged it perfectly. They come in and first have Oli stop them while he plays a creepy tune on a keyboard. Then they see me sitting on a table wiggling my legs and screaming. Followed by another guy who violently gets tossed around the room (he was knocked out cold more than once). Followed by another guy running behind them looking like Leatherface with a chainsaw.

In this room we made little kids, teenagers and young adults pee themselves. One guy threw up. One kid actually shit himself. There were countless screams and actually traumatized expressions.

It was perfect.

I finished out that haunted house season with an endless supply of new friends who respected that I was so comfortable with my situation (none of them had a clue how nervous I was in the beginning). I earned a new sense of glorified confidence in my body image and my whole self. I no longer cared about the staring. Just like a light switch, it just shut off. Eventually I stopped noticing people staring altogether. The scars on my legs and skin graft scars were no big deal either. It all added to the image. I was learning to play my hand and minimize my limitations for the first time since I had my amputations.

I worked with that same haunted house group for four years, even regularly driving back for my shifts across the state after I turned 18 and left my hometown. It was one of my best and most cherished experiences ever. It's impossible for me to think of that haunted house and not smile to myself. The light I experienced at that time still shines through me today.

I found that light by facing my fears. I had to turn the most negative reaction I had ever suffered into the very thing that I wanted most from people. I had to dive into that darkness to find the light hidden underneath. I had to embrace my fear, my self-doubt—even the depths of my own disgust—to realize that there was a massive benefit when the perspective shifted.

It's a good example of how a mind-set changes from living in darkness to living in light. The circumstance was the same; people were still staring whether or not I was crawling on the ground, on a table with horror make-up, or at a grocery store. Now, I saw it as a benefit. I was able to flip my mind-set and because of that I went from darkness to light.

The other benefit here was that my new friends weren't scared to recognize the humor in my situation. I have heard nearly every cripple insult or gimp joke out there. From them asking if I have enough leg room in a car to them pulling pranks on me, like putting beer on top of the fridge as their way of cutting me off when I drank too much (to be fair it was often deserved as I took a while to discover my limits). It might sound cruel but honestly, I welcomed it. Sure at times it got old if it was nonstop but 99 percent of the time I simply reminded them they were jealous their dicks weren't longer than their legs and told them to shut up. Whether or not they realized it, each of them played an important role in helping me feel comfortable in my skin.

Life in light is a place that must be earned. Rarely does it just fall into our laps and let us run with it. It is a constant work in progress to maintain the mind-set where all things are possible and all things can be—even are—beneficial. But goddamn, is it worth it! It is our greatest possible accomplishment because everything that follows is good, beneficial and beautiful.

Just as darkness can have two meanings, so does light. Living in light can be another way to say "living in comfort." This isn't a particular example I have a lot of experience with and when I do, I try to shun it away. Comfort is necessary at times, sure, but growth comes from darkness. Growth comes from living on the other side of fear. The light I found with the haunted house wouldn't have been available to me if I stayed comfortable, sitting at home and playing video games or doing whatever else I did at that time.

In this way, life in light is enjoyable, yes, but a life that is always "in light" will not allow personal growth and transcendence.

You have to embrace the dark to discover the light. They go hand in hand. They always will.

Chapter Sixteen

KNOW THYSELF

"To know thyself is the beginning of wisdom."

—Socrates

THIS IS THE LAST YEAR YOU'RE GOING TO BE FAT.

That all too familiar voice in the back of my head, my daemon, spoke to me as I looked into a mirror on January 1, 2020. I stared myself up and down. My love handles tipping over the ends of my wheelchair. Solid C-cup man-boobs. And a look on my face like I was absolutely fed up with life. Something needed to change. Whatever version of life I had experienced thus far was subpar to what it could be, and hanging onto all of this extra was holding me back.

About time, I thought.

This was about a year and a half after Kendra. My healing process was rough, still trapped in the nightmare space in my head.

The year after Kendra (2019), I met someone new. A short relationship but one I look back on fondly. Her name was Taylor.

Taylor didn't do anything specific; I'm an independent adult in every way now and then. But she did remind me that I had value as a person. I was worth listening to. I was worth caring for. I was attractive. She showed me all of this simply by being there. She listened. Doesn't sound like much, but for me this was everything at that time. I like to think we needed each other for the time we did, but not everyone is meant to be forever.

Wherever she is, I wish her well.

That relationship gave me the small piece of confidence I needed to get my life together again. It had fallen apart since Kendra and I wasn't making the progress I felt I could have.

I'd say I suffered from obesity my entire life, but to do so would put the burden on a disease as opposed to something I did to myself. My obesity wasn't something anyone placed upon me. No one ever force-fed me anything, outside of split pea soup from my dad when I was younger (it was *disgusting*). I made the choice to regularly order out. I made the choice to use food as a coping mechanism for my own discomfort. I chose this lifestyle, which reflected an undeniable lack of self-respect and lack of personal worth. Saying I suffered from obesity isn't right. Saying I allowed myself to be obese seems to fit more precisely.

In 2019, I hit my top weight of 265 pounds. If I had legs, this would've looked more like 380 pounds at nearly six feet tall. I remember seeing that and being shocked. I hadn't weighed myself in a while and my lack of clarity around my eating habits was staring directly back at me on the scale. I felt disgusted with myself. I had never surpassed 250 before that, or so I thought.

The progression took a couple months. I started off with a ketosis diet but couldn't keep to it. Years ago in grad school I discovered macronutrients (macros). I lost 40 pounds with this method before I stopped tracking them and regained it all in a couple months. I decided to go back to that method after months of failed ketosis.

Even better (for my diet), COVID hit. COVID shut down the live entertainment music industry for about 18 months. I used this to my advantage in that I couldn't use the excuse of not having time to meal prep. I also quit drinking for diet purposes.

For the first five months of macros tracking, I lost 10 pounds per month. Fifty pounds in five months is impressive by any standard. I'd like to say I was a cheerleader to myself on the way down but somehow my self-critic turned into Milo Yiannopoulos.

Know why Kendra cheated on you? Because the other guys didn't suffocate her with their gut every time they fucked her. Your titties were almost as big as hers, fatso.

You want to eat that? You fat fuck! Why? So you can be a fat fucking loser for the rest of forever? Go for it. You remember how much fun you had wiping sweat off your underboob?

No one cares if you miss flavor! Welcome to being an adult! Not every meal needs to be the tastiest ever. You'll live, you overindulgent fat, greasy, gross bitch.

Around month three it dawned on me that there was no end to this. There was no more *just make it one more month*. This had to be a true lifestyle change. This is when the voice became motivating.

You got this, bro. Come on! You lost 50 pounds in five months. That's fucking incredible. Let's keep getting it! Not there yet!

See? Cooking ain't so bad. Long as you get and stay in your groove, this is just normal routine now. You got this!

Do not stop! You got more in you! Do not quit! Do not give up! You are better than this. Fuck this exercise! Get it!

Over the next seven months, I lost another 30 pounds, totaling 80 pounds of weight loss in a year. A couple months after that, I got skin removal surgery. The loose skin was excessive. It looked like an oversized T-shirt on a thin mannequin. I was incomparably more insecure in my body with my skin being loose than I ever was with being fat. This insecurity created a race to the finish line feeling in me. Understandable, but it worked against me. It made me forget what I remembered around month three: There was no end to this.

Unfortunately, the eating problem wasn't fixed. This was shown to me in grand fashion when I was healing from surgery. I ate excessively, shittily, and with no regard to keeping my weight down. The time I should have been most cautious of my diet was after I had skin removal. A high level of carbs in your diet will bloat you. Bloating is the last thing you want when 11 pounds of skin was recently cut off your body. I healed terribly, busting out stitches because I was putting on weight again.

Even with an impressive 11 pounds of skin removal, I knew I would need to go back for a round two one day. I was 50 percent body fat for a prolonged period of time. There was simply too much for the doctors to safely take at once.

Eventually I healed, and even though I had some new scars, I never felt better about myself. It didn't just feel like 80 pounds of weight loss and skin removal. It felt like my old life was behind me. All of the bullshit, the self-hate, the lack of self-esteem was gone. It was like I couldn't see it anymore. My physical look represented my internal feeling.

Plus, all those years in the gym (and TRT, of course) allowed me to pack on quite a bit of muscle size. I felt like a teenager in the football locker room. Every time I saw myself in the mirror I did a Terry Cruz chest flex.

My chest was impressive now instead of depressing. Let me enjoy it!

After losing all that weight, I realized many things about myself. First, I had never felt more accomplished or elated in my abilities than when I was able to keep the weight down and off. Something I had tried to do my entire life and always failed was finally accomplished. I was never more in love with my body, life choices, and career than I was in September 2021.

I never really learned a strong sense of discipline. This isn't to say I hadn't practiced discipline in other areas of my life, but when it came to eating it was nowhere to be found. Emotional eating was something that started at a young age. When no joy was to be found, there was food.

Feeling down? Order from Mike's Pizza in Fort Lauderdale. A salad, a large pizza, and a slice of cheesecake. Girl you were crushing on denied you? Rocco's Italian Eatery has one of the best subs I've ever eaten in my life. Got high tonight? Gas station across the street has chips and ice cream.

It's cool, though, I'll roll there and back. That'll make up for it, I'd think.

Being disciplined is all about telling yourself, "NO!" It's about keeping to a goal. It's about maintaining the sense of integrity that you have with yourself. It's about trusting yourself, keeping to your word, and being loyal to your own goals. It's a day-in-day-out promise that you hold close and don't break for short-term gratification. It's being in control of your emotions. It's developing a sense of emotional intelligence. It's shadow work. It's facing harsh truths and realities that you will no longer ignore.

It's stoic. It's esoteric. It's Divine.

None of this is even touching on the outside perception that people have of those who are fat. I can astutely state that there is a true prejudice against the obese. Whether it's deserved or not is for you to decide. I can say that as my own weight started to drop, I had a change in perspective of the obese. I always saw someone's weight as their responsibility. Even with medical issues there is a multitude of things you can do to maintain your health. I don't have legs, used a wheelchair for nearly 21 years, and I figured it out.

Save the excuse for someone else.

Regardless of this idea, I went from disgust, part of which was undeniably my own, to pity. I would see someone well into morbid obesity and wonder what had happened in their life that made them feel like that was okay. I see some old photos of me and the first thought that pops in my mind is: *What happened that made you think this was okay?*

The number of people I heard taunt and criticize the overweight dramatically changed. I went from hearing something every now and then to regularly hearing those around me feel some kind of way toward the obese. I wondered how many times I was the subject of these conversations over the years.

On a lighter note, people seemed to receive me better. Was this because I was happier with myself? Absolutely. But the number of people who smiled at me saw a noticeable increase. The women who seemed interested in me shot up. The work opportunities that I came across improved with force. Sex in shape versus obese was unmatched. My walking ability saw an unknown ease. My other workout performances revamped.

I even got my petty revenge rejection. A woman who used to turn her back to me every time I came around her friends was now asking if she could come by after the bar closed. With this change in my own body, my standards changed as well. Plus, self-respect comes into play here.

I never responded. And it felt *so* good.

Every fat person knows this desire. You can sit there and act like you're above it. You're not. You have/had it, too.

Okay, lesson learned. Being healthy beats obesity for any given reason any day of the week.

Noted.

Although I didn't see it at the time, this was the beginning of my separation from Satanism. After my skin removal, my perspective on indulgence was different. I also understand I distorted LaVeyan concepts.

Indulgence instead of abstinence is a great idea; but unchecked, this becomes an overindulgence. Like anything else you could overindulge in, an addiction pattern begins to be created. The habit starts to get built. Eating every time you're depressed is no different than masturbating excessively or doing drugs when you're depressed. It's a self-sabotaging method you use to cope. Maybe if you eat enough, or drink enough, or relieve yourself, then you'll feel better. Then you'll feel full. Then the pain will go away.

It doesn't. That's not how that works.

Truth is, to truly navigate that space you need to show up with consistent discipline. It is one of the most difficult goals for people who have these coping mechanisms, but it is a necessity nonetheless.

Satanism is not a rejection of discipline. Even with the summarization of *indulgence instead of abstinence*, Satanism in itself is not anti-discipline. I think the idea would be that an adult would already have this part of their life figured out prior to discovering the philosophy. I wasn't so lucky. I found Satanism at a young age. I didn't develop the disciplined nature to adopt this kind of lifestyle.

In diet terms, it's like intuitive eating. Intuitive eating is listening to your body for what it needs for nutrition. To do this you'd have to know your body and its cues extremely well, and it only works if you've had a consistently healthy diet for a prolonged period of time. If you haven't had a consistently healthy diet, your body will crave the junk you've been feeding it.

If you eat cookies every day and then try to intuitively eat, you'll desire cookies every day.

In the same way, I was practicing indulgence without an understanding of when and how to use it. There is a right and wrong time to practice indulgence in a variety of ways. Occasional drug use won't bring me back to 2017, whether it's psychedelics, weed, or booze. Occasionally loving myself won't turn me into my porn addict days. Occasionally eating shit won't bring me back to the habits I had when I hit 265.

I know this now because I learned it through my weight loss journey. I navigated amputations when I was 11. I forced myself through various opiate withdrawals, almost always having more of them within reach. I spent years, buckets worth of sweat, wearing my body constantly down to hit my bench personal record of 350 pounds. But learning to consistently meal prep over ordering out?

Impossible. The hardest thing I've ever done in my life was lose that 80 pounds.

Worth it in every way. So much so that I judge my level of self-discipline on my weight now. I found that correcting this problem created discipline in other ways. My time management improved. My confidence improved, not just for the aesthetic, but for finally knowing I had this part of my life under control.

With each passing year I embrace the new me and kill the underdeveloped clone.

While I'm sure Socrates would like to take credit for "know thyself," it was actually a saying within the Hellenistic culture long before him. The idea of "know thyself" might just be the groundwork phrase for the Left Hand Path philosophies.

Through knowing yourself you can understand where you exceed and where you are limited. LaVey, Crowley, Blavatsky, Greaves, and a variety of various pagan-based myths all have referenced a direct message of "know thyself" in some way.

With understanding where you exceed, you can further take the LaVey/Rand route of a life dedicated to fulfilling your ego. With understanding your limitations, you can work to improve them, partially through your ego but spiritually as well. This is where Luciferianism, Buddhism, and Theosophy can take you but LaVey and Rand cannot.

A big part of knowing yourself is understanding your personal duality. To look back on your life and accept not only what happened to you but what you chose to do. To understand your own *why* and explore it for a while.

When I look at my younger self, my old actions, and lay them out I can appreciate the best spiritual advancement one can gain from . . . life.

I understand it's easy to armchair-quarterback someone else's decisions and lifestyle. It's not hard to sit back and judge. We all do it, myself included. I can and have looked at friends and family and thought something they did was absolutely retarded. I have looked at the decisions of other people and said to myself, *There's no possible way anyone could be this stupid*. People have done the same about me.

Shit, I've done it to myself.

It's easy to look at all of this and negatively judge. "You're a moron for getting your truck slammed into when you were 16." "You're ridiculous for calling God 'Lucifer' and believing in many gods." "You're a criminal." "You're an addict." "You're less than me."

You can say all of the above but you weren't in these situations. The vast majority of you had no effect on them. You are not me. I am not you. You weren't there, in the moment, just as you weren't there in all the moments that led up to the decisions I made. You were not as challenged as me. And conversely, I was not you during your own trials and tribulations.

Reminding myself of this, reminding myself that I go through life with the daemons I recognize and the philosophical and ethical structure I've built, keeps me grounded even when others will challenge me. I've found if you can turn down the noise in your head caused by someone else's voice and look at your life, your choices, they will start to make sense. It all comes together in a sometimes beautiful, sometimes ugly, jigsaw puzzle of your life. And piece by piece you can put it all together and understand it.

I stand behind every decision I've made. Doesn't mean I'm proud of them all—I'm most definitely not. But I can look at every situation I've been put into or placed myself in and stand behind it. It took all of this and more to know myself. It took a total understanding of my own humanity to find pleasure and joy in my past and present, along with hope for my future.

A good way to understand this is to look at your past. Really work to understand it.

Enjoy the duality . . . should you be so daring to have one.

ACKNOWLEDGMENTS

My sister and her family—Not only were you the first editor I used, you're also pretty cool. Ditto your family. You kept this sinister project a secret from our family before it got published and for that, I think you're at least half to blame for our family now being attached to these devil worshipping ideals. Maybe mom or our brother could've talked me out of it. I guess we'll never know . . . All thanks to you, big sis!

My brother and his family—Are we brothers? No . . . Yes! Classic line from one of the dumbest movies ever made but it fits, seeing as I am clearly the most handsome son and because of that, you've always been jealous you weren't as pretty. I know this has been hard to accept throughout your life, but it's okay. You still scored an awesome and beautiful wife and you two made a really cool daughter. Appreciate your wins, bro.

My mom and stepdad—I hope this reads clearer now as to what it is that I believe, why, and how I practice it. I feel like there was some confusion. And you never said it but I got the impression you were upset there wasn't more of you in here. I hope the point I made about 'if it isn't relevant to the topic, I didn't write about it' explains that. On the flip side, not only did I give you a starting chapter quote, I credit you as the first person to make me realize I missed my mark.

Keeping me humble since '91.

Thanks, mom . . .

Keyleigh James—Some time has passed since your death and you're still a regular thought. I think about what was happening while this book was being written, and everything after, and how much I would've appreciated your insight. Because of this, like your brother said at your funeral, my kids will miss their Uncle Keyleigh, regardless of not being able to meet you.

Lynn Picknett—If I have a daughter, at some point she will learn about feminism in school. While Susan B. Anthony and Michelle Obama are important feminine leaders, so are you, and she will know that. You courageously challenged the status quo. Your research is—in part—responsible for a worldwide discussion on religious history and the importance of feminine divinity being recognized. It has been an honor for me to work with you . . . both times.

My prosthetist and her team—There aren't many people in this world that I have encountered that I would say embody the term "angel," but my prosthetist and her team have certainly proven to me that they do. She has worked countless hours with me to help me walk and I will be forever grateful for her kindness, advice, and guidance in my journey.

1106 Design—Your guidance has taken this book from an idea to a reality. I greatly appreciate your help and input throughout us working together . . . all three times.

ABOUT THE AUTHOR

HENRY "PANIC" PANICCIA works in the music industry as a concert promoter, artist manager and tour manager. Paniccia received his bachelor's degree in history and minored in political science. He then went on to graduate school where he obtained his entertainment business master's degree.

Paniccia began studying theology, specifically Abrahamic religions and the proposed counter, occult philosophy, when he was just thirteen years old. Fascinated with the cultural implications that religion and philosophy have played throughout history, he continued to learn about these ideals into adulthood, eventually finding solace in Luciferianism.

FOLLOW HIM ON SOCIAL MEDIA!
Instagram-Twitter-YouTube
@HENRYPANICCIA

If you enjoyed this book, please leave a review online.
It is much appreciated!

www.ingramcontent.com/pod-product-compliance
Lightning Source LLC
Chambersburg PA
CBHW020522080526
44583CB00013B/706